P9-BYS-672

Megaliths and Their Mysteries

Megaliths and Their Mysteries

A Guide to the Standing Stones of Europe

Alastair Service and Jean Bradbery

Macmillan Publishing Co., Inc.
New York

Copyright © 1979 by Alastair Service

All rights reserved. No part of this book may be reproduced or
transmitted in any form or by any means, electronic or mechanical,
including photocopying, recording or by any information storage and
retrieval system, without permission in writing from the Publisher.

Macmillan Publishing Co., Inc.
866 Third Avenue, New York, N.Y. 10022

Library of Congress Cataloging in Publication Data
Service, Alastair, 1933-
Megaliths and their mysteries.
1. Megalithic monuments—Europe.   2. Europe—
Antiquities.   3. Neolithic period—Europe.
I. Bradbery, Jean, joint author.   II. Title.
GN776.2.A1S47   936   79-20977
ISBN 0-02-609730-3

First Printing 1979

Printed in the United States of America

Contents

Frontispiece – the huge stepped cairn of Barnenez on the north coast of Brittany (see page 67).

Preface and Acknowledgements

Anyone who, like us, has been visiting and reading about megalithic sites for many years, will have been intrigued by occasional references to similar structures in other parts of western Europe. Were they constructed by the same people? Was their architecture linked? Did they share religious preoccupations and a study of astronomy? These and many other questions kept recurring. Yet it took a good deal of research even to discover the whereabouts of many of the important megalithic sites. The general books on the subject all concentrate on Britain and Brittany with some references to Malta and Spain, despite the overall sweep of works such as *Ancient Europe* (Piggott 1965, etc.). So we set out to produce an illustrated guide to the great megalithic structures throughout western Europe, noting the different types, and what they had in common. During the past three years, one or both of us have visited the main sites described.

We have given a summary of the archaeological evidence and theories as we understand them, and have also aimed to give a brief account of many new theories and interpretations suggested by other disciplines. We have used the generally accepted archaeological terms and names, except where these seem to imply interpretations which we do not accept (for example, we have used the term 'chambered mound' rather than the archaeologists' 'chambered tomb' since we do not believe that these monuments were used solely – or even chiefly – as tombs). Lastly, we have given our own view of the many levels of meaning expressed in megalithic structures and of the underlying themes common to all of them.

Many people have helped us in preparing for the book and we thank them for all they have done. Among them, we must mention John Cox, who has given a great deal of help on astronomical matters, as well as Inga Aistrup, Andrew Davison, Richard England Sant Fournier, Sonia Harmer, Mrs G. Horton, Selwyn Hughes, John Irwin (whose researches on the primeval mound are central to our conclusions), Andrew Kerr,

Lisbet Koch-Olsen, Karl-H. Krause, Elizabeth Leader, John and Sorrel Lister-Kaye, Judi Marcell, John Michell, Peter Payne, Gerald Ponting, Jill Purce, Susannah Raby, Christine Le Moing de Tissot, and the staff of the Institute of Archaeology library. We must also thank Professor Alexander Thom for his helpful comments on the introduction in draft, though we should make it clear that he does not accept the ideas about dowsing, leys and the like, of which we have given an account.

All the photographs are by Alastair Service, except plates 30 and 31, which are by Jean Bradbery, and plates 69 and 70, which are by Inga Aistrup.

Note on Dating

Most of the dates given in this book have been arrived at by recently developed scientific techniques, although some are the result of archaeologists' cross-dating with similar products from some other place: in the first case the dates are usually expressed as, e.g., *about 3100 BC* or *around 2400 BC;* in the second case they are given as, e.g., *thought to be about 3700 BC*. In both cases the dates should be treated with caution, for several reasons.

Scientific dating of prehistoric sites employs three main techniques. Pollen from plants survives an extraordinarily long time and its age can be established by complete analysis. The thermoluminescence present in all pottery deteriorates at a fairly constant rate from the time the pot is fired, and so the age of the pot can be measured. All organic matter contains carbon-14 (radiocarbon) which decays gradually from the moment life ceases and after more than 60 000 years disappears. The stage of decay can be detected by chemical analysis of the proportion of radiocarbon in the material and so the age of the former organic matter is discovered.

All these main methods, and others, are subject to considerable margins of error – at best they give dates accurate to a century or two either way. The first radiocarbon dates were published in 1949 in New York and by 1955 the system was generally accepted by archaeologists. In 1967 an American professor of chemistry, H. E. Suess, published a paper comparing ancient radiocarbon dates with the annual tree-rings of an exceptionally long-living Californian tree called the bristlecone pine. Before 800 BC, the tree-rings showed that its wood was older than the radiocarbon date it gave. This error increased in tests on older wood to a point where tree-rings of 5200 BC gave radiocarbon dates of only 4200 BC. The reason for the error was found to be that the proportion of radiocarbon in the earth's atmosphere, previously assumed to be constant, has varied over the millennia as the earth's axis tilted; radiocarbon originates from a bombardment of the earth by atoms beyond the solar system, and the tilt of the axis permits varying amounts to enter the atmosphere at different periods. Correction or calibration tables were published and, as with the announcements of the first radiocarbon dates themselves, these calibrated dates showed that the megalithic cultures of western Europe were much older than archaeologists had previously thought. Ideas that they were influenced by old stone structures in the eastern Mediterranean and farther east – which could be dated from written records – had to be abandoned.

It is not known whether further errors in the radiocarbon technique, or in those of pollen and thermoluminescence dating, will yet prove that the present accepted dates are still wrong by centuries. However, it should be said that the different techniques now seem to be showing a reasonably consistent pattern.

One other caution is needed as regards the dating of megaliths. Thermoluminescence and radiocarbon dates are obtained from material found in the monuments, not from the monuments themselves. There is no known way of measuring when boulders, whose rock is millions of years old, were put in their present positions – unless a datable object was buried under the rock at the time of construction. Occasionally objects are found under the foundations of megaliths which probably date from their erection (charred wood and burned seeds give the best radiocarbon dates, while bones and horn can be used but are less consistent). But usually the dates are from objects discovered in or near a megalithic chamber. In these cases it is impossible to be absolutely certain that the megalithic monument was not built long before the object was put there. Equally, it is possible that the monument was rebuilt or enlarged over objects which had been placed there much earlier.

The radiocarbon dates in this book have been calibrated according to Professor Suess's curve published in 1970.

Introduction

The word megalith comes from the Greek, and means a great stone. It is commonly used of any structure built of large stones, usually set upright in the earth, and dating from 5000 to 500 BC in western Europe.

The commonest kind of megalithic monument in Europe, generally called a dolmen, is a chamber formed of upright stones (sometimes called orthostats), with one or more large flat capstones laid across them, to make a roof. These were often originally covered with a mound or cairn, but not always, and many of the covering mounds have now disappeared. Some of these chambers, instead of capstones, had a corbelled roof, that is, a vault formed by smaller, flattish stones, arranged in overlapping layers. The dolmen is called an anta in Portugal, a stazzone in Sardinia, a hunebed in Holland, a dysser in Denmark and a cromlech in Wales – and many other local names. They are found from the heel of Italy to the north-west of Ireland, from the south of Spain and Portugal to Denmark, and southern Sweden. In many of them traces of human burial have been found – others seem never to have been used for burials, and we are interested in exploring some of their possible uses.

The other kind of monument which occurs throughout most of Europe is the single standing stone. This is often called a menhir, especially if it is large, and not part of a group or structure. It is sometimes carved or partly shaped, but some appear quite rough-hewn. Some of these menhirs have been shown to have a possible astronomical function, as a marker or foresight. Their other uses are only just beginning to be deciphered. They are at once the simplest and most enigmatic of megaliths.

Alignments, long lines of standing stones, are also found from Denmark to Corsica. Some stand close together, others stretch for miles across the countryside. An astronomical use has been clearly demonstrated for several alignments, especially those at Carnac in Brittany, the largest and most famous of all. They also suggest ritual uses.

Circles or rings of standing stones are found in hundreds across the

British Isles, where they seem to have been preferred to the close-set alignments of other countries, though in Cornwall circles and alignments (of a much sparser and more extended kind) occur close together. But stone circles, in their local forms, are scattered in small numbers through Denmark, Belgium, France, Czechoslovakia, Portugal, Sardinia, even Menorca. Nineteenth-century antiquaries also mention

Fig. 1. Areas of western Europe where various types of megaliths occur, dating from between 5000 and about 1000 BC. The names of major groups dealt with in this book are marked. Dolmens of various sorts or rock-cut chambers are found in almost all areas, but in southern Germany only menhirs are recorded.

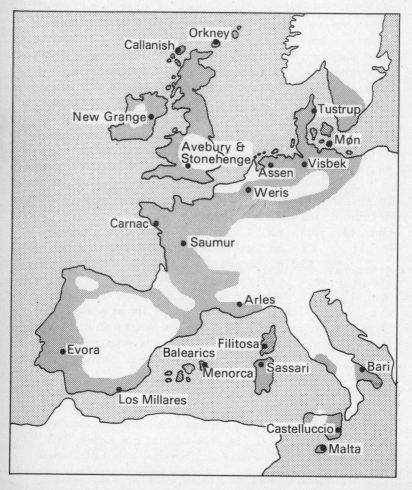

them in other countries such as Switzerland and Italy, but we have not found any direct evidence of these. Again, many of the British circles have been studied, and their astronomical significance clearly shown. And again, they seem very clearly built for ritual use, too.

There are other megalithic monuments which can only be loosely grouped together as sacred enclosures. In northern Europe the commonest kind of enclosure is a raised quadrilateral – often hundreds of metres long – with rows of standing stones along its sides: these earth platforms invariably have burial-chambers towards one end, but their size and orientation suggest other uses. In Brittany there are stone kerbed quadrilateral enclosures which do not contain any kind of mound or burial-chamber; sometimes a tall menhir stands near them. There are many rare, very localized forms in Britain, Denmark, Germany, Holland, France, Corsica, Sardinia and the Balearics. And, of course, quite unique and deservedly famous are the temples of Malta, with their clusters of lobed spaces.

Yet another type are the rock-cut chambers. These occur throughout Iberia, southern France, and the western Mediterranean islands, often on a very grand scale. Most seem to have been used as tombs, but some were lived in.

Lastly, there are the earthworks, some of considerable size, which must have taken huge resources to build. These are often an integral part of the stone monuments – the ditches and banks of Avebury and other great circles; the broad terraces of the Maltese temples; and the great mounds over the chambers of Newgrange, Maes Howe and the Cueva de Romeral. Man-made mounds often seem to have a central role in megalithic lay-outs. Some, like the Tumulus St Michel at Carnac, hold minor burials; others like the majestic Silbury Hill in England, and Monte d'Accoddi in Sardinia, do not.

Other sacred hills, if not man-made, were certainly shaped by man. Glastonbury Tor is one of the best known, and is of that half-pear or yoni shape often found, and almost always topped by a sacred tower or spire now – as if at some time it was imperative for Christianity to put its mark on these hills. Their sides are often ridged, and this ridged form has been seen as a spiral path or three-dimensional maze. There are a few surviving turf or earthwork mazes, which may go back to megalithic times, and we see these, too, as having a sacred purpose. These hills and mazes are linked to our theme, but it is beyond the scope of this book to cover them in any greater detail.

We have described the main types of megalithic works, but there are many other kinds, and many local variations. Stone houses and huts survive in a few places. Fans of small standing stones spread across the ground in northern Scotland and in Brittany. Avenues of double rows of standing stones seem to provide a processional way in some places, sometimes progressing in curved lines across the countryside. A new type of drystone walling of large blocks, usually called cyclopean masonry, was developed in Malta in 3500 BC and – with no apparent connection – two thousand years later in Sardinia. The Sardinians used this technique to build huge round towers; similar towers are also found in Corsica and the Balearics, which these people conquered. Their colonists built many sorts of megaliths unique to each island – the most notable are the Taulas in Menorca.

Megaliths throughout the rest of the world

This book sets out to cover only the works of a particular period in western Europe, but there are of course many monuments in other parts of the world which can be described as megalithic – some of these date from different periods. Elsewhere in Europe there are standing stones north of Istanbul on the Black Sea coast of Turkey and of Bulgaria, while some later Ionian monuments have similarities (and used to be thought the ancestors of those in western Europe, before radiocarbon dating proved otherwise). There are many standing stones of unknown age in north Africa, especially in Algeria. One theory about the origins of the megaliths in Europe is that African colonists met eastern Mediterranean settlers in Iberia, and their meeting stimulated the development of the new type of structure in Portugal and Spain (MacKie 1977, 162).

Further into Africa, Glyn Daniel reports megaliths in the Sudan and Ethiopia. In America there are standing stones of various types around the Gulf of Mexico, while the Polynesian Islands have many monuments which could be called megalithic. In Asia, they are found in Palestine, Caucasia, Iran and Baluchistan. Farther south, there are megaliths in Assam, in Kashmir, central India and southern India – where the stone chambers of Mysore and the Deccan have been dated to the Iron Age between 200 BC and AD 50. They exist in Sumatra and there are many in Japan. The great Ishibutai tomb has a passage 38 feet (11.6 metres) long, leading to a big chamber 15 feet (4.6 metres) high, roofed by two capstones estimated to weigh over 60 tons each. The building of megalithic monuments in Japan was finally forbidden by the Emperor's decree in the seventh century AD (Daniel 1958, 20). Denis

Roche adds to this list reports of standing stones in Korea, Tibet, Sri Lanka, Madagascar, the Crimea, Bolivia and Peru (Roche 1969, 164).

The development of megalithic design 5000–500 BC

In most European countries, building of megaliths began several centuries after the introduction of farming. The earliest traces of settled farming, rather than the roaming life of the hunter gatherer which went before, have been found in the Levant, around the eastern Mediterranean, dating from earlier than 7000 BC. It reached Palestine in about 6500 and Egypt around 5000 BC (Renfrew 1973, 61). Forest clearance, and cultivation of that cleared land, probably started along the coasts and rivers of southern France and the Iberian peninsula by 5500 BC. The first megaliths in the south appear to date from about a thousand years after that – from 4500 BC in Portugal, perhaps 4000 in southern France, and in Malta, farmed since 5000 BC, from about 3700.

In northern Europe, the last Ice Age released its grip in about 10 000 BC. For the next 3000 years a gradually receding bridge of land joined Britain to the Continent from Denmark to Normandy. Varying dates are given for the rise of farming in these northern countries. On the islands of Téviec and Hoëdic off Brittany are the remains of pre-farming communities, dated from 5500 to 5000 BC (Renfrew 1973, 143). But the earliest Breton megaliths have been dated at 4700 BC. In Denmark, traces of the first farmers have been dated at 4200 BC (Dyer 1972, 8), and the first dolmens known there were built about 3500 BC. Cultivation in the British Isles seems to have started a little later, and the earliest associated monuments have calibrated radiocarbon dates of 3700 BC at Knockiveagh in Ireland, and 3600 at Maumbury Rings in England. These farming people seem to have travelled by sea or river, rather than land, and settled near navigable water. Extensive clearance of the northern forests did not begin till about 3000 BC – since the main tools used by these Neolithic people were of flint, antler or wood, it is not surprising that they cleared only when growing numbers made it necessary.

From all this, it is clear that the earliest megaliths were built in Brittany and Portugal, at about the same time, before 4500 BC, and in the next thousand years similar monuments went up in Denmark (and probably north Germany), the British Isles, parts of France outside Brittany, Spain and Malta. Apart from chambered mounds (sometimes surrounded by stone circles) and other megalithic chambers, it was only in Malta that anything considerable was built during this early period – the great temples.

Here it is worth looking at the climate of northern and western Europe at that time. Scientists have recently been tracing prehistoric weather patterns from a study of plants, insects, snails and other animals found in many sites of different periods (Evans 1975 and Lamb 1974). From the end of the Ice Age the sequence seems to go like this: from 9500–8500 BC (Pre-Boreal period) the cold gradually diminished, allowing first lichens and mosses, then birch and pine trees to grow; from 8500–6500 BC (Boreal period) increasing warmth and dryness saw oaks and hazels flourishing; from then until about 4000 BC (Atlantic period) heavy rain and high temperatures encouraged the growth of deciduous trees on high ground which is open moorland today, and elms and alders joined the earlier forest trees. Spain and Portugal were probably at their most fertile towards the end of this moist Atlantic phase, and this may partly account for the early development of a megalith-building culture in the south of both countries.

The next period – 4000 till roughly 1400 BC (Sub-Boreal period) covers the whole of the Neolithic, and much of the Bronze Age in north-western Europe. In these years (except for a time of wet weather around 2900 BC) the climate was warm and fairly dry. High ground could be cultivated after the clearances, which left the horizons open; the skies were clear for observation; the sea was usually smooth for sailors. Today, not many would choose to live in a fragile hut near the megaliths on the wild moors and heaths of Cornwall, the Outer Hebrides, northern Jutland or Wildeshausen – but four thousand years ago it would have been comfortable living and good farming. This is the period when people began trading much more widely, travelling far greater distances. With this, the exchange of ideas speeds up, too – new artefacts and new kinds of structure spread fast – perhaps by word of mouth, perhaps through colonization.

During the earlier half of the Sub-Boreal period the great monuments include Tustrup in Denmark, many chambered and circled cairns in Scotland, Newgrange in Ireland, the causewayed camps, Wayland's Smithy and the long barrows in England, Gavr'inis and many large chambered mounds in Brittany, the massive Loire dolmens, the rock-cut chambers near Arles, the Cueva de Romeral in Spain, and of course the Maltese temples. Spain produced a phenomenon, too, at the end of this period; the Millaran culture, founded on the wealth of its early copper mines long before metal was used in the west of Europe generally.

After the break in the fine northern weather around 2900–2800 BC came a fresh surge of innovation. A new kind of pottery is found all over western Europe, dating from 2500 BC onwards. Copper, and later, bronze implements gradually replace flint. Some archaeologists believe this is all to be explained by new techniques spreading across the Continent, but most see it as evidence of a new people – the Beaker folk (after the characteristic new pottery associated with them), who colonized or took control of the native populations. Assuming that they were one people, there is still some doubt whether they came originally from central Europe, or from Spain. One widely held theory is that they were relatively small in numbers, but that their knowledge of the sun, moon and stars, and of farming and building, established them as ruler-priests in many Neolithic communities.

Whatever the origins of the Beaker culture, its spread coincided with the last gigantic monuments of the Neolithic peoples and with the beginning of new ideas in megalith building. The giant stone circles such as Avebury, Stenness in Orkney and the second monument built at Stonehenge were started early in the period after the weather cleared again – before the Beaker people arrived. By the year 2000, the Carnac alignments and Great Menhir observatory were probably started.

Other alignments such as those at Wéris in Belgium and Sartène in Corsica may be of similar dates, while the intersecting circles of Li Muri in Sardinia (and similar circles in Corsica) are also of that time. Strangest of all are the solitary menhirs in large areas of Europe – they are rarely datable unless material is found under them, but they seem to be associated with this period.

While all these exciting new developments were going on, the megalith builders, or their ideas, were still spreading, and dolmens, with their mounds, were still being built in many parts of western mainland Europe, reaching the heel of Italy, and the Mediterranean islands. These dolmens were either the chambered sort called 'passage graves' by archaeologists; or the type in which the passage is itself the chamber, called 'gallery graves'.

The third monument at Stonehenge – the great Sarsen ring and trilithons of 2100 BC – was the last giant circle. After 2000 BC the drive of the circle builders in the British Isles, under the influence of the Beaker people, seems to have been towards quantity rather than size. About nine hundred small circles are known in Britain and Ireland. This may be seen as providing for the religious needs of a growing population, or as indicating more specialized kinds of local astronomical observations (Burl 1976, 137–53). Dolmens and mounds went on being built in some places, rock-tombs were being cut, alignments and men-hirs were probably still being erected, and many other less common types of monument appeared all over Europe during the five hundred years before 1500 BC. One of these is the remarkable Monte d'Accoddi in Sardinia, a 'high place' built of cyclopean drystone, which in struc-ture seems to be a precursor of the later towers of the western Mediterranean. From this time too came the statue-menhirs of Corsica.

Then the climate changed again. After 1500 BC it became markedly colder and by a century later the Sub-Atlantic period had set in through-out northern Europe and as far as central France. This cool and wet Sub-Atlantic weather is still with us in the twentieth century AD.

The effect of the worsening climatic situation was dramatic for the megalith builders and their astronomers. A thousand years of celestial observations could not be continued, for the sky was now clouded over more often than not. The high open country became a miserable place to live and it was at this time that the peat moss, encouraged by the damp, started to accumulate in layers over the previously fertile upland soil. The farmers must have moved to lower and more favourable land, if it was available. The circles and alignments were probably deserted from this time – no more appear to have been built after about 1500 BC in northern Europe. Less certainly, the same appears to be true of dolmens – the latest calibrated radiocarbon date from a French dolmen seems to be about 1400 BC for St Georges de Levezac.

In the Mediterranean the story is different. In most of the mainland areas, the megalithic cultures seem to have lingered on, without further development of their monuments, until Phoenician, Greek, Carthaginian or Roman colonists subjugated them. It would be easy to see these areas as outlying survivors of a loosely connected megalithic culture, now deprived of its centre in northern Europe.

One Mediterranean island, however, appears to have produced from about 1500 BC onwards a last flowering of the megalithic era and an unco-ordinated empire of its own, just as the rest of western Europe was moving into another age. The tower-building people of Sardinia, sometimes called the Shardana, seem to have emerged from the native population of the island (perhaps aided by some new arrivals) and to have fitted themselves formidably for the warlike era which followed the comparative peace of the great period of the megaliths. These Tower People soon dominated their own island and then invaded and held Corsica and the Balearics for about a thousand years. They were farmers and warriors, and in each of their dominions they developed quite new sorts of monument particular to each island. The designs and structural techniques appear to be rooted in the earlier European megalithic tradition. But their Giants' Tombs, Taulas, Navetas, Nuraghi and other forms are an impressively original finale to the long story of megalithic architecture. That story ends finally with the Roman conquest of Menorca in 23 BC.

The people who built megaliths – sailors and navigators

The megalith builders, or most of them, had spread by sea to their early settlements in western Europe. A look at the map of their distribution in Europe shows that they built for the most part along the coasts or along easily navigable rivers, and had a special liking for islands and groups of islands. An oar of fair size from northern Europe has been radiocarbon dated as early as 8000 BC, while there are rock carvings which seem to represent ships of between 3000 and 1000 BC in Malta, Brittany and Scandinavia. Pottery of all megalithic periods shows every sign of cultural contact between the various parts of Europe. In the calm seas of the Neolithic and early Bronze Ages, boats were a far quicker and safer method of travel than overland. And a knowledge of navigation and the tides would in itself provide one reason for studying the movement of the stars, the sun and especially the moon.

Farming and food

The sun and moon provide the calendar for farming, which was practised by all of these people. The early farmers of around 4000 BC grew wheat and barley in their forest clearings in northern Europe – examples have been found in many places as far north-west as Denmark, and the islands around Scotland, throughout the following thousand years. Millet, spelt and perhaps oats have been found in an early site in Belgium. They herded cattle, sheep, goats and later pigs, their preference depending on local conditions. Wild boar, red and roe deer were hunted in the Netherlands, birds were caught in some places. Many of them gathered shellfish and some caught fish from the sea or rivers – recent excavations at Skara Brae have revealed the remains of cod and coalfish, both bottom feeders in the sea. Grinding stones were used to make flour so that some form of bread could be baked. Flint knives and scrapers were used to prepare the animal carcasses and fish. To this diet of bread and meat and fish, they added eggs and local fruits – raspberries and apples have been traced in middens in Denmark as early as 3000 BC. The climate was warm and the land only thinly peopled – living must have been reasonably easy once the forests were cleared.

In southern Europe, farming had started perhaps a thousand years earlier than in the north. East Mediterranean farmers were herding goats and sowing barley and early forms of wheat called emmer and einkorn before 7000 BC. Cattle were kept long before 6000 BC. Farming techniques spread along the African coast and the northern Mediterranean to Italy and Spain by the year 5500. In central Portugal and in Andalusia, the early people ate the meat of oxen, goats, sheep and pigs, while wheat grain of this period shows that the people around Valencia ate bread of sorts. By about 4000 BC, rye had been added to the wheat, while olive stones and grape seeds in the habitations show the ancient use of these fruit in Spain. In Malta the temple builders of around 3500 BC had been growing barley and club wheat and emmer for well over a thousand years. They also ate the meat of pigs, cattle, goats and sheep. By 2500 BC the Ozieri people in Sardinia were varying a diet of the same grains and meats as the Maltese – wild boar, deer, rabbit, hare, horses and even foxes appear in their rubbish dumps.

Clothing

In sites in the Netherlands associated with the Danubian culture, and dating from before 4000 BC, the imprint of primitive matted textiles has been found, but woven textiles came later. The Sardinian Ozieri people seem to have had woven clothing around the year 2500, for spindle-whorls and parts of looms have been found in their domestic sites. All the earliest spindle-whorls seem to come from the time just before the arrival of the Beaker people (one of about 2500 BC was found at Durrington Walls henge in England) and even then they are extremely rare finds in most of Europe. Woven cloth was probably very unusual and special until perhaps 1800 BC. From this time there survives the woven, woollen clothing of a blond man found in a barrow at Muldbjerg in Denmark – a belted robe going over one shoulder, and under the other, a round cap and a fine full cloak. Vegetable fibres were mixed with the wool in these garments, and a body found at Kellythorpe in Yorkshire was wearing a robe of nettle fibres. The early clothing of men and women was probably of leather, which may well have been carefully scraped and cured, to judge from the many suitable tools which are found. It is possible that some of these clothes were painted or stained, or even patterned and embossed with designs like those on the pottery of the time, but these clothes have not survived, and only the Danish finds give a clue to the shape of their robes. But we do have plenty of evidence of the manufactured ornaments which these people wore, of many different materials. There is no reason to think that they went about bundled in rough skins, and the fatuous 'imaginative' drawings so often seen, which show great megalithic structures being built by shaggy 'neanderthals' are absurd.

The people who wore these clothes, four thousand years ago, were of

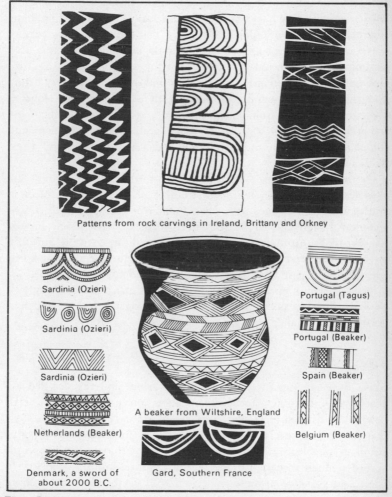

Patterns from rock carvings in Ireland, Brittany and Orkney

Sardinia (Ozieri)

Sardinia (Ozieri)

Sardinia (Ozieri)

Netherlands (Beaker)

Denmark, a sword of about 2000 B.C.

A beaker from Wiltshire, England

Gard, Southern France

Portugal (Tagus)

Portugal (Beaker)

Spain (Beaker)

Belgium (Beaker)

Fig. 2. Patterns associated with the megaliths.

many different physical types. Many had the long skulls typical of northern Europe today, but others were of stockier and more round-headed kinds. It is clear that the megalith builders were a scattered culture made up of many peoples, rather than a race.

Houses

Comparatively little remains of the dwellings of the northern peoples after they moved out of caves and rock shelters. In southern Europe, the lower stages of many huts have survived, usually circular, and of stone. Impressions found on lumps of clay show that the upper parts were of wattle and daub. This may well have been the kind of construction used for huts in the north too. Examples of villages are known at Le Lizo near Carnac, at Geelen in Holland – with timber Long Houses of before 4000 B C – at Troldebjerg in Denmark – with its 200-feet Long House of about 3000 B C made from wattle and daub, and round huts about it – and at Skara Brae in Orkney. Skara Brae is a pre-Beaker settlement, and contemporary with the Stenness circle and Maes Howe mound a few miles away.

Of the Beaker people's settlements, in northern Europe, there are even fewer remains. In the small number of places where traces of houses and small villages have been found, for example on Dartmoor and near Lough Gur in Ireland, only shallow post-holes of circular houses survive. Again, fine weather probably made heavy walls unnecessary and soil erosion may have worn away all but the deepest post-holes. All the same, there must have been storms and colder winters, so the evidence remains puzzling. It is likely that many more remains of these dwellings lie under the blanket of peat which grew over much of northern Europe after 1500 B C.

Sages and rulers

Skara Brae's houses of stone are great rarities and this has led archaeologists and others to speculate about the nature of the special people who lived in them. Both in Orkney and in Malta there are signs that there was a special caste of people, apart from the general population, in sizeable megalithic communities, even before the Beaker people spread through western Europe in the centuries around 2500 B C. In Malta, the skeletons of those associated with the temples after 3500 B C indicate a lightly-muscled people, who ate a special diet which wore down their teeth very little for Neolithic times. The bones of animals slaughtered at an uneconomically early age, and other clues at Skara Brae, where the inhabitants lived in houses luxurious for the time, point to a group whose skills and status entitled them to be supported by the ordinary people, without manual labour, around 3000 B C. In many other parts of Europe the small numbers of skeletons found in megalithic tombs compared with estimates of the total population can best be explained by the theory that these were reserved for a special group in the community – whether they were hereditary rulers, or priests, or scientists of the time.

One theory which has been strongly argued (Renfrew 1973) is that local family territories, with a chambered mound or cairn as their central religious or cult monument, gradually combined in some areas to form larger 'chiefdoms'. The Isle of Arran in Scotland has been given as an example of a group of family territories – the seven very early dolmens east of Evora in Portugal might well be another. Instances of possible chiefdoms are Malta, with its six pairs of temples seen as centres for populations of one to two thousand people each, and Wessex in England – where six chiefdoms may each have been based on a causewayed camp such as Maiden Castle's first stages in the south or Windmill Hill near Avebury in the north. This theory sees stone circles in Britain, close-set alignments in Brittany, and other monuments elsewhere as developing independently and gradually replacing the earlier chambered mounds or temple-tombs as the settings for seasonal religious and communal gatherings. It is an alternative to that older idea that each new development in the building of the megaliths was brought by a new wave of people, either from the east, or from Spain.

Together with the start of the Bronze Age, in the centuries after 2500 B C, the Beaker people appeared. They mingled with existing communities in some parts of Europe; in others they established separate colonies near existing settlements. And at this time the hints of a ruling caste continue. The new culture introduced small round barrows, and in some places closed up the huge Neolithic barrows, which had been used for collective burials for generations. In the round barrows of the Bronze Age, people were buried singly or sometimes in couples of both sexes. Weapons, especially battleaxes, appear in these round barrow graves and very occasionally there have been gold ornaments among the bronze. The famous 'chief' excavated at Kellythorpe in Yorkshire, showed every sign of being a warrior king. There is no certain way of knowing whether in the apparent unrest of the Bronze Age, the rulers retained the spiritual and scientific knowledge which probably gave them their authority in calmer Neolithic times.

Astronomy and the megalith builders

So much for a description of megaliths, their builders and their physical background. Most of this information has come from the archaeologists. When we look at the use and meaning of these structures, one view is that because of the human burials frequently found in them, they must all have been primarily funerary structures. This is reflected in the names given – chamber tombs, burial-mounds, passage graves, gallery graves, etc. But some archaeologists themselves are beginning to question this, and to look for other interpretations. And here other disciplines can enormously enrich our understanding – mythology, comparative religion, art history, anthropology, and others. Apart from burials, the clearest evidence we have is for their astronomical use. Alexander Thom, the former Professor of Engineering at Oxford University, and his followers, have established that most of the non-funerary monuments could have been used as lunar observatories.

Today we see the movements of the sun, moon, planets and stars with a picture in our minds of our earth within the solar system and the stars beyond. Megalithic men and women did not *necessarily* have any such picture and to understand the movements of these celestial bodies, simply as observed from earth, is a matter of extreme difficulty. The planets are seen to move in wilfully convoluted paths, and there is no trace of a megalithic observatory which tried to cope with an understanding of their patterns. Many alignments of stones on stars of great magnitude have been suggested – allowing for their changed positions over four thousand years. A star-clock for the night time is a possibility, though unproved.

The sun's annual pattern is the easiest to follow. It soon appears to an observer that the longer the sun's passage, from its rising to its setting, the warmer the season. Thus by noting, at any one place on the earth's surface, the point on the horizon where the sun rises each day, a pattern of the year is readily detected. The rising place is well south of east at midwinter, but moves steadily to north of east in summer and then back again. The setting point similarly moves from south of west to north of it, and back again. When the sun rises due east and sets due west, the daylight hours are as long as the darkness and this is called the equinox. At midsummer and at midwinter there are several days of apparent standstill, when the sun rises and sets in the same places. This sequence of changes appears to people on earth to cause their cycle of seasons. Apart from being the subject of a study proper to any revered object, the sun could therefore provide a calendar for each year's events – the movement of animals for hunters, the growth of distant wild crops for gatherers, the timetable for cultivated crops and herding, and the dates of the regular festivals.

Such are the sun's seasons as seen by mankind. What is actually happening is that the earth's axis tilts towards the sun in the summer and away from it in winter, so that summer comes to the northern half of the globe when it is winter in the southern half. Now, the earth's orbit forms an ellipse around the sun, which it takes a year to traverse. Seen from the side, however, that orbit is along a flat plane, which is called the ecliptic. The earth's axis of spin, between the north and south poles, might be expected to be at right angles to that plane. In fact it is not, and the angle at which it differs from a right angle to the orbital plane is called the obliquity of the ecliptic. This angle alters with time. In 4000 B C it was $24.11°$, in 2000 B C it was $23.93°$ and at the present time it is $23.5°$. This alteration has to be taken into account when detecting the use of prehistoric observatories.

The moon's behaviour in the sky, if watched from earth, is much more complicated. While the earth is orbiting the sun in just over 365 days, the moon orbits the earth every $27\frac{1}{3}$ days. But the moon's orbit is not in a fixed plane as regards the earth – it rotates in a shifting pattern which broadly speaking, is repeated every 18.61 years. This period is called a lunar cycle of 18.61 years – there are other lunar cycles of different periods.

Twice in each lunar month, the moon's orbit cuts across the plane of the ecliptic. These crossing points are important in lunar astronomy – they are called the nodes. After every three lunar cycles of 18.61 years, i.e. every 55.83 years, the pattern of the nodes is completed and recommences.

Once in every lunar cycle of 18.61 years, the moon reaches its greatest apparent height – as seen from earth – at the peak of its passage through the sky and for over a year it continues to reach approximately this height once a month. This period is called the moon's major standstill. A subsidiary effect of the major standstill is that a fortnight after its peak each month, the moon rises only to a very low point in the sky. We shall see later in this book that at the northerly latitude of the earth's surface on which stand Orkney and Callanish, off the coasts of Scotland, the high trajectory produces the extraordinary phenomenon of the moon appearing scarcely to set, while during its low trajectory it seems to move along only just above the horizon. An observer from a latitude as far north as Shetland will see the full circle of the moon's circumpolar path clear of the horizon during the high trajectory.

The other important event in the moon's cycles is the minor standstill. This occurs nine years after the major standstill in each lunar cycle of 18.61 years – for several months the moon appears to reach the same low maximum height in the sky each month.

A study of the moon, whether she was considered a goddess or not, would be natural to people who moved on the sea, as the megalith builders did. Not only does the moon affect the tides, with their exceptionally high and low Springs and Neaps, but a knowledge of her movements in the sky is of great value in night navigation. If she was a deity to these people, it would be important to foretell when and where she was going to appear during their rituals. In many civilizations, a lunar calendar was adopted, with a year of 354 days (corrected by an occasional year of 284 days) – the Romans used a lunar system until Julius Caesar reformed it to the solar method, while the Jewish and other calendars are still moon-based.

A combined knowledge of the movements of the sun and the moon would enable the sages to predict the occurrence of the most dramatic of regular natural phenomena, the eclipses, which would provide a focus for ceremonies to celebrate the moment when the light was reborn. Eclipse prediction requires advanced mathematics and lengthy record-keeping. The basic knowledge needed is of the cycles of sun and moon, especially the lunar cycle of 18.61 years and its triple period of 55.83 years, when the patterns of the nodes are repeated. The achievement of such standards of mathematical skill and record-keeping by a people who apparently did not write used to cause many scholars to doubt the evidence of megalithic astronomy. It is now generally assumed that some of the records were kept by memorized repetition in the ritual day by day, while other information may have been marked on wood now decayed beyond recognition. It is possible, though less likely, that carvings on rocks and stones may contain a coded record which has not yet been understood. Some incomprehensible settings of standing stones in various places may themselves be a tabular record, while posts or ropes within stone alignments and circles could be devised for this purpose.

It is likely that the first megalithic monuments later used as observatories were not built for observational purposes at all. Archaeologists have found that stones were often moved from their first positions in circles. We have come to believe that early chambered mounds were probably oriented towards the midwinter sunrise for symbolic spiritual or ritual reasons – perhaps so that the reborn sun could bring its re-vitalizing power among the living people gathered in the forecourt and into the chamber of the dead. Early studies of the sun could be carried out from the mounds – the circles around some of them may have been connected with this purpose. The development of the rites and of the study of the moon could later have made people realize the need for additional structures away from the chambered mounds – certainly in Britain there is a frequent pattern of early circles built near major barrows.

The moon observatories are thought to have emerged around 2800 BC. The first structure at Stonehenge dates from that time and was not aligned on the midsummer sunrise. Its earthworks and post-holes have been interpreted as the remains of markers covering a series of cycles of the moon – totalling about 110 years – which would be enough to confirm the existence and regularity of that cycle of 18.61 years. The Aubrey holes around the outer bank of the monument may also have been connected with this work. It is tempting to guess that this feat may have established Stonehenge as a centre of lunar studies, which would account for its unique series of reconstructions during the following thousand years and more.

Observations of the sun continued to be refined in various ways at many different places in northern Europe. At Kintraw and at Ballochroy in Scotland, Alexander Thom has pointed out that in about 1750 BC – still in the period of fine clear weather – standing stones beside plat-forms on the hillsides could be lined up with notable mountain peaks many kilometres away in such a way that the midwinter sun and the mid-summer sun respectively would set behind them. Such long sight-lines would give a very accurate reading of the sunset's position. But the principal object of study was the moon, and some observatories appear to have been both solar and lunar by this comparatively late period.

Various types of lunar observatory were built from 2800 BC onwards and the detection of their functions has been the special achievement of Thom. He and his followers have established that most of the non-funerary megalithic monuments which they have examined in Britain and Brittany could have been used for this as well as ritual purposes. Later circles may even have been used *only* as observatories. It is quite possible that when such researches are extended to Denmark, Germany and other countries with megaliths, similar astronomical functions will be traced.

Lunar laboratories were built in various sizes and forms. It has been found that the type of great earthwork avenue called a Cursus – the best known is near Stonehenge, but the longest is the six-mile-long Dorset cursus – aligns at various points with horizon markers that indicate the rising or setting places of some important phase of the moon. Single menhirs could be used similarly in conjunction with barrows or with notches dug in distant hillsides on the skyline.

The most splendid of these observatories were undoubtedly the alignments, aligned enclosures and circles of standing stones of around 2500 BC which can be found in some parts of western Europe. Of this period, these are far more monumental than is needed for their purposes as observatories (Avebury, the second and third Stonehenge phases, Arbor Low and Stenness are good examples) and this suggests they served as ceremonial centres as well as scientific laboratories.

One of the dozens of lunar sites which Thom has analysed carefully is a complex called Temple Wood, near Kilmartin in Argyll and just three miles (five kilometres) from the sun observatory at Kintraw. There is a stone circle and a strange setting of thirteen stones, five of which form the plan of an X on the ground. From various of these stones, noticeable notches in the horizon would have lined up with the setting moon at important stages. The same lines can be worked out at many stone circles and other sites. Again, some circles and other monuments have outlying standing stones to provide the key line for observations, which could have been of major stars as well as moon risings and settings. More rarely, a central stone aligned with one of the ring may indicate a key point on the horizon. Tall single menhirs may have been used as distant foresights for observations from given positions. Assuming that these fixed sights pointed towards a rising or setting point of the moon at an important stage, observers would check their calculations by lining up the moon precisely with the foresight, moving a few paces to one side of the backsight each night as the orbital pattern moved along the horizon. The correct point of observation might be marked by a post in the ground and a series of such points would be recorded during the following nights. This information could then be used for extracting further indications of great importance about future eclipses, although it would be subject to error unless put through some process of extrapolation, as we shall see below. In France and elsewhere there are many alignments which were perhaps used in similar ways to the British circles, while

Germany has over one hundred recorded solitary menhirs and France many more.

Apart from calendar observations, the chief reason for all these prehistoric astronomers' most intricate night-time work is thought to have been the prediction of eclipses. For this purpose, the coincidence of sun, moon and earth in a straight line can be foreseen by watching the pattern of the moon's nodes (when it passes through the plane of the earth's ecliptic), by observing when the moon rises opposite to the sun's position, and by noting the 'minor perturbations' of the moon – these are caused by the gravitational pull of the sun which distorts the pattern of the moon's path. When minor perturbations are at their most extreme, eclipses of the sun are most likely. But to predict an eclipse precisely, Neolithic men had to work out when the moon was at its maximum declination (declination is the equivalent, in the sky, of latitude on the earth's surface, that is to say, it is the angle expressed as a number of degrees above the equator of an imaginary sphere, called the celestial sphere, around the world). Having found the time of the moon's maximum declination, a rule of thumb can be worked out and applied to predict eclipses of the moon and even, more approximately, of the sun.

To observe the moon's maximum declination is simple enough if it is reached when the moon happens to be visible to the astronomer. But it may well be reached when the moon is out of sight. Thom believes that it was to make this difficult calculation, by marking a succession of nightly observations and then extrapolating a curve to indicate the maximum point which might fall between the markers, that the fan settings of stones in north-eastern Scotland and parts of the great alignments of Carnac were laid out.

Thom envisages the rows of stone fans being used almost like graph paper, so that the astronomers would hurry from their observation points and plot their nightly findings – using either one of the stones as a marker or a rod thrust into the ground in the appropriate place. When the series of observations was complete after several days, some sort of rope or hide strips could be laid out describing a curve which took in all these points. Parts of the Carnac rows might be used in the same way, by plotting sightings made at the observatory centred on the major Manio menhir near Kermario or at the huge observatory which is thought to have had Er Grah, the great broken menhir, as its central foresight. Certainly, part of the Petit Menec alignments at Carnac is very like the Scottish fan at Mid Clyth. Various different methods of extrapolation have been detected in other places (Wood 1978, 129–39).

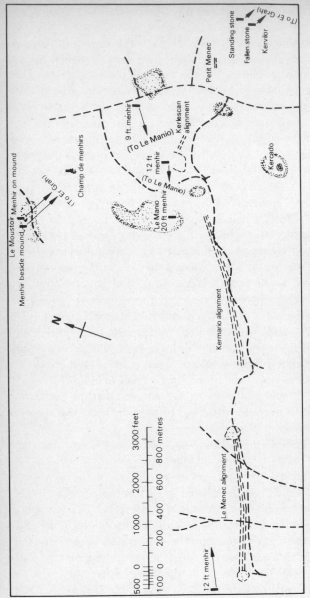

Fig. 3. The Carnac alignments, showing the nearby standing stones which could be used as an observatory employing the 20 feet (6.2 metres) high Le Manio menhir as a foresight. Others could be used as part of a larger-scale (and thus more accurate) observatory employing the 60 feet (18.5 metres) Er Grah menhir (now broken) at Locmariaquer as a foresight. These observations could then be plotted with wooden stakes on parts of the great alignments and forecasts could be made of astronomical events. (Plan derived from Alexander Thom.) See Fig. 7.

After carrying out the extrapolation, the exact point of the moon's maximum declination could be found and any forthcoming eclipse could be predicted. It should be noted that this function would employ only small parts of the Carnac alignments and certainly would not have needed the massive stones found at the western ends of each. The explanation for the monuments as a whole must be sought elsewhere – as in other megaliths, scientific uses seem to have been integrated with ritual design.

Professor Thom's work, and that of his pioneering predecessors in the last century, was considered unsound for many years until the sheer weight of his published research convinced all but the most conservative archaeologists that the general theory, if not all its detail, is correct.

Megaliths and geometry

There are more than 900 stone circles in the British Isles, from Bodmin Moor to the Hebrides, and from Wiltshire to Donegal. Professor Thom's researches have shown a common unit of measurement – the megalithic yard, 2.72 feet in length. This megalithic yard also fits the geometrical patterns which can be traced in the structure of many megalithic monuments. These patterns are discerned by students of sacred geometry, an ancient science concerned with the mathematical relationships and harmonies which underlie the whole universe, and which express the laws of its functioning, from the largest scale, the macrocosmos – to the smallest, the microcosm. The principles of this science are manifest in the description of Solomon's Temple in the Bible, as in the dimensions of the Great Pyramid; in Pythagorean teachings on divine harmony, as in Renaissance architecture; in the master works of Islamic architecture, as in the great medieval cathedrals – these teachings were at the heart of the masons' secrets.

On the large scale in the European landscape, great areas of central Germany have been interpreted as being laid out so that ancient sites are on straight lines hundreds of kilometres long and these lines in turn form geometrical shapes whose dimensions are in certain magic proportions – many of these seem to display geometrical qualities first published by Pythagoras (Gerlach 1942–3, 11–13). In England, a remarkable straight line has been traced from St Michael's Mount in Cornwall through Glastonbury and Avebury to Bury St Edmunds in Suffolk; while another runs north–south from the major Arbor Low stone circle in Derbyshire through Avebury and Stonehenge. Both these lines miss absolute straightness by a few hundred metres at one or two points, but that does not alter the fact that they are remarkable findings over such distances. Further huge geometrical figures have been traced over southern England. An isosceles triangle, with Arbor Low at its peak and two sides of approximately 151 miles, straddles Wessex and the Midlands. A decagon based on the line between Glastonbury Abbey and Stonehenge takes the patterns from Wessex into Wales, while a heptagon has been discerned as embracing Wessex itself with two southern points that would only have been on dry land before 6000 BC (Behrend 1975, 9).

On a smaller scale, regular polygons and stars have been found in the geometry of stone rings (e.g. Critchlow 1977, 25–30) underlying the egg shapes or flattened circles which are the commonest overall shapes found in the British rings. At Odry in Czechoslovakia a group of eight stone rings, with five nearby man-made mounds, form lines that seem to

Fig. 4. The primary leys of England. The St Michael Ley from St Michael's Mount to Bury St Edmunds, the north–south Ley through Arbow Low and Stonehenge, and the isosceles triangle with Arbor Low at its apex. The lines are accurate to a few hundred yards, but the significance of Mersea Island is not clear and the sides of the triangle which should be equal are not quite so. Lines similar to the English leys have been traced in Germany.

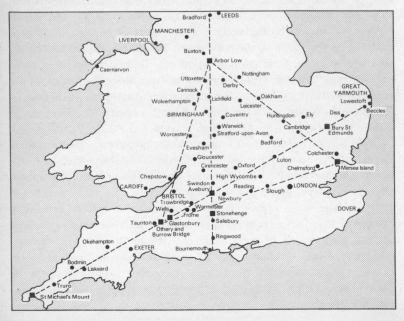

indicate a knowledge of true east–west and north–south in about 2000 BC (which is confirmed by other megalithic sites) and significant geometrical relationships with each other. Some of the great dolmen chambers such as Crucuno at Carnac have also been analysed as being built with symbolic proportions.

Further research may reveal whether such measurements and lines were designed intentionally or arise by chance, though perhaps these ideas are not susceptible to proof in present scientific terms.

Megaliths in their landscapes

Yet another system of lines detected in the countryside seems to have links with a worldwide form of geomancy less rigorously mathematical in its approach. We have noticed while visiting megalithic sites all over Europe that they are usually, though not always, sited so that the countryside falls into certain patterns around them. The classic megalithic site is on a platform part-way down a spur which runs from higher ground behind. From the site itself, a bowl or valley in the land will be noticeable below, while the horizon will be surrounded by ridges of hills which wrap around behind the spur. These hills will be seen to run along about three-quarters of the skyline, but the rest of it will be more open. Since the countryside in which megaliths were built varies a good deal – though it is never completely flat and very rarely truly mountainous except in the distance – this layout can be seen on quite different scales. At the monumental Knebel ringed dolmen in Denmark, it is at its most dramatic – as it is at Li Muri in Sardinia, Los Millares in Spain and Filitosa in Corsica. It is equally evident, though in a much gentler form, at Callanish in Scotland, Forrières in Belgium, Ggantija in Malta, Stonehenge in England, Monte d'Accoddi in Sardinia and most other sites of importance. It is even discernible in the low curves around some of the hunebedden of Holland, where they are not too densely surrounded by trees. It was not mandatory, for major mounds such as Newgrange in Ireland and Kercado at Carnac are sited at the very tops of their hills, as is Hagar Qim in Malta. But it is so common that coincidence seems out of the question.

For an explanation of this systematic siting of megaliths one may turn to a book by an English missionary to China in the middle nineteenth century AD. This clergyman, E. J. Eitel, noted down all he could discover about an ancient and just surviving geomantic science which the Chinese called Wind and Water (in Chinese, Feng Shui). Textbooks on the subject dated back to the thirteenth century AD Sung dynasty, but Eitel noted that its origins were much older (Eitel 1873, 7). According to this science, which is based on a subtle conception of the order of nature far from our own today, there are currents – perhaps magnetic, Eitel hazards – within the earth's surface. Like electricity, these have positive and negative aspects, male and female, which the Chinese symbolized as the azure dragon and the white tiger. These dragon and tiger lines flow through the landscape and, in the angle close to where they cross and temporarily combine, 'there may be the luck-bringing site' if in the same place there is also 'a tranquil harmony of all the heavenly and terrestrial elements', including the direction of the water courses (Eitel 1873, 23). Now, the happy site is almost always sheltered by the hills, slightly elevated within them, and connected to them by land through which the geodic currents flow. In the angle formed by the junction of such hills, the geomancer looked for a 'little hollow or little mound', from which the chains of hills around can be seen to form 'a complete horseshoe' with one side open, and with streams that run away gently rather than steeply. In China, geomancy was employed to find the best sites for tombs, temples and houses. There was much more to the Chinese geomancer's art than has been described here and his equipment included a complicated compass from which to read off favourable and unfavourable factors. It is clear that this approach does tend to select the same kind of position as that chosen for so many megalithic monuments by Neolithic builders four or five thousand years ago (Cox 1978).

Most people, at some time, have experienced particular places as specially benign, or happy, and others as dismal, threatening or evil. Some churches feel holy, others quite blank, yet the quality of the architecture does not seem to be the sole explanation. The report of 1972 by the English commission on exorcism convened by the Bishop of Exeter, explains many of these experiences as 'place memories', associated with events that happened there. This may be the case, but it seems to us from our own experience that there are naturally sacred places. E. A. S. Butterworth, writing of the Greek mysteries, speaks of the trance-like state being 'induced with peculiar ease in certain places' (Butterworth 1970, 99). It is possible that Neolithic men and women not only shared these experiences, but had an understanding of how to find such places; of the lie of the land associated perhaps with some special union of earth and sky. The more of their sites one visits, the stronger this impression grows.

What may be another ancient way of assessing such sites is being explored today – dowsing – sometimes called water-divining. This practice, often dismissed as quite without scientific foundation, persists because it works.

From the 1930s onwards, French and English dowsers have noticed that they picked up very powerful reactions from the ground around megalithic monuments. Some of these were like the movements of the instrument felt over underground springs – yet no spring was there when excavation was done, so these places were dubbed blind springs. Similarly, paths across the fields could be traced, which reacted like subterranean streams. A dowser called Guy Underwood worked in the field for many years on these traces and his findings were published posthumously (Underwood 1969). He noted three sorts of invisible track which dowsers can detect – these he called water-lines, denoting an actual stream, track-lines, which were weaker and often followed paths, and aquastats, which run in pairs and override track-lines. Most extraordinary of all, he noticed that megalithic sites, especially stone circles, tend to be meeting-places of all these types of line. The plan shows the lines which he traced around Stonehenge, many of them

Fig. 5. Patterns formed by primary dowsing lines under the ground at Stonehenge and its surroundings, as recorded by Guy Underwood in his 1954 book. Note the typically spiralling formation of the lines at their ends.

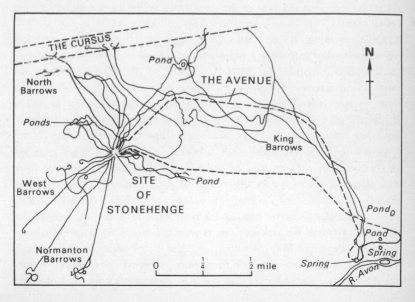

ending in ponds or spiralling inwards to end in blind springs.

More recent dowsers have pointed out that these lines are not constant – they change over a period – but the megalithic site remains a centre for them. They have also concluded that what they receive is in part an 'electromagnetic radiation' but also has another less tangible component (Graves 1978, 16–22). Many of them have continued Underwood's experiments with megalithic structures and have produced some strange findings which require confirmation, but should be mentioned briefly here. First of all, some dowsers do not feel *any* of those lines around megaliths. Others, however, have found an effect of concentric rings of underground charge radiating from the centre of stone circles. These searchers have also noticed an electromagnetic charge in standing stones themselves, and find that this tends to be divided into seven bands if the stone is over five feet (1.5 metres) tall. Five of these bands are above the ground, at heights varying with that of the stone, the middle one above the soil being the strongest (one dowser even claims to have been knocked over by it). The dowser Tom Graves tested these charges regularly at the Rollright stones circle in England for a week, and found that only twelve of the seventy stones kept the same charge throughout – the rest changed frequently, sometimes from hour to hour. These qualities have been ascribed to the presence of quartz in most megalithic stones. Finally, some dowsers now claim to have received impulses along the straight lines between megalithic and other ancient sites, which are known as ley lines.

Leys are straight lines running through, and marked by, standing stones and other megaliths, earthworks, pools, mounds, and various landmarks, such as notches on the skyline. Over smaller distances they have been traced and recorded by many people in the countryside of Europe and beyond. John Michell's careful research in Land's End, Cornwall, revealed many alignments of stone rings, standing stones and barrows covering up to seven markers in straight lines several kilometres long (Michell 1974). In Germany, such a system of straight lines was noticed in the 1920s by a clergyman called Wilhelm Teudt, who believed they had astronomical purposes (Teudt 1929). In England during the same decade, and quite independently, a businessman called Alfred Watkins detected similar lines throughout the country, which he believed were a network of tracks for travellers marked across the largely forested prehistoric valleys and hills (Watkins 1925 and 1927). Watkins called these leys, because they pass through numerous places whose names end with the syllable ley. Ley-hunters now see these lines not so much as physical tracks or roadways, but as paths for some sort of current or energy. This is sometimes described as 'earth-energy', sometimes as telluric or geodic current, and appears to be, at least in part, some sort of electro-magnetic force. There have been attempts to measure this, as a deviation from the local geo-magnetic field, but this work is barely begun. We see this current that the dowsers react to as the same force that the Chinese geomancers use, and it can best be understood by referring again to the Chinese concept of Chi (or Ki in Japanese). This energy is seen not only to flow through the planet, but all living organisms. Chinese traditional medicine has made a special study of this Chi in the human body; the paths or meridians along which it runs; and ways of correcting imbalances in the flow, by acupuncture – that is, by inserting needles at appropriate points on the meridian, to restore smooth running. Western medicine, while not recognizing the theoretical model, is coming to acknowledge that, in practice, somehow, it works. In the martial arts, the Chinese and Japanese, by working with this Chi in the movements of the human body, can surpass mere physical force and weight.

The ley lines then, form part of this network on the planetary scale. The megaliths are seen as not only marking this flow, but in some way directing or channelling it. The great monuments are built on points where this force is particularly accessible, so that rituals performed there at the right moment, as shown by the sun and moon, will promote a harmonious flow in both earth and people.

Rock-carvings and symbols

Here a look at the carvings associated with megaliths may help elucidate their purpose. The best modern book on the megalith builders' carvings (Hadingham 1974) concludes that they date from between 3400 and 1200 BC in Britain and demonstrates that the same types of pattern appear in various areas of Europe generally quite separate from each other. Thus the cup-and-ring marks – concentric circles with a round hollow at their centre and often a line penetrating to it – are found in Spain, in Britain only north of a line from Anglesey to the Wash and throughout Ireland; there are particular concentrations in central Scotland and in south-west Ireland. Plain cup marks at stone circles are concentrated in eastern Scotland, carved chamber-mounds are most commonly found in eastern Ireland. The great megaliths of southern England and Holland have barely a carving between them. Carnac has many rock carvings but with the exception of Gavr'inis – which has designs similar to Irish,

Ireland

Sicily

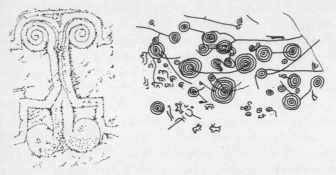

North-West Spain

Northern Scotland   Malta

Fig. 6. Neolithic rock carvings of spirals and cup-and-ring marks from various parts of Europe.

Maltese and Spanish types – the motifs are almost unique to Brittany. Cup marks are fairly common in Denmark and northern Germany, but very rarely with rings. It has been pointed out that the largest complex carvings usually appear on natural outcrops of rock, rather than on megaliths.

It is a confusing situation, which confirms one's suspicions from the distribution of passage- and gallery-type dolmens that many sub-cultures or religious variations existed within megalithic Europe. All the same, widespread motifs do exist. These include the cup-and-ring marks, spirals, spoked wheels, zigzag and serpentine lines, and concentric arcs and whorls. Most of these appear on Neolithic or Beaker pottery in various parts of Europe, but the spoked wheels, the spirals and the cup-and-ring marks hardly ever do so, if at all. This seems to indicate a special significance for them. The spoked wheels are usually interpreted as sun-symbols, and this seems likely enough since the earliest wheeled vehicles known in Europe only date from a little before 2000 B C in Hungary and had solid wheels (Piggott 1965, 92).

The spirals and the cup-and-ring marks are more elusive. Spiral patterns are associated with the cult of the Great Goddess, who was worshipped around the Mediterranean as bearing and nurturing all life. In North America the Hopi Indians called the spiral the Mother Earth symbol. In Australia various tribes see spirals as the path of 'the Totemic ancestor himself, in his capacity of food producer'; concentric circles are said to mark his stopping-places. There are many other similar interpretations from other parts of the world, all referring to a primary life source, and sometimes referring to its path. In some of these cultures it also carries the sense of the original, underground, cave sanctuary from which these people believe themselves to have emerged into the world. In another, perhaps more esoteric sense, the spirals, arcs and finger-print motifs are associated with passing beneath yokes, forks or porticoes; or being drawn through an ancient stone gate; the pathway between the worlds; the passage through the magic arch, the gate of death and rebirth; passing through a state of death into a state of life (Neumann 1955, 292; Varagnac 1968). So the suggestion here is of rites associated with initiation, and with personal transformation.

The spiral also describes one stable form of flow of all energy – the vortex ring, as we can see it in the movement of water and smoke. This spiral form is the basis of the movements of all the martial arts, which work specifically with the energy flow of the body. And we can see this movement expressing itself in living organisms and their movements all around us (Schwenk 1965; Jenny 1967). Each of us has experienced this in our own bodies before birth, slowly unfurling during the nine months of gestation. This spiral expresses the expansion and contraction which is the nature of life.

The 'cup-and-ring' marks, or patterns of concentric circles, are closely related to the spiral in their meanings. Where the spiral may represent the path of the life-bringer, concentric circles may stand for stopping-places on that way. Where the spiral refers to the Great Goddess, so too does this concentric sign, symbolizing the belly or womb from which all life comes – and more specifically, the belly and navel (Neumann 1955, 132). It is also seen as representing the navel of the earth – the omphalos. E. A. S. Butterworth in *The Tree at the Navel of the Earth* calls it the omphalos-sign. This idea of the omphalos used to be thought of as comparatively late, arising from Ionian influences. But it is now seen as very ancient and very widespread (Butterworth 1970, 37). Within this concept of the omphalos, there is also implied an umbilical cord, an invisible link reaching from the depths of the earth, through the navel, right up into the heavens (Roscher 1913, 12 and 23 ff). This fits very well with the idea of megaliths as places of interchange between the cosmic forces of sky and earth.

These images of the navel and the invisible cord are closely linked with another theme which is central to the understanding of megalithic monuments. This is the theme of the pillar and the mound, which in different versions underlies creation myths from many different cultures. The core of it seems to go like this. Before things began floating on the undifferentiated waters, an island or mound forms, wandering. Some heroic deity impales the mound, with a post, tree, nail or pillar. As this mound is pierced, fixed in one place, so heaven and earth fly apart. Light and dark, and all other dualities are polarized: rushing to fill the void, space comes into being: from that movement of space, the four cardinal directions emerge. And so the matrix is formed for the whole physical universe. Human beings celebrate and re-enact this nailing of the mound to affirm and ensure the order of things, to keep the pillar, the axis mundi, in its place. This act is embodied in sacred structures all over the world (Butterworth 1970; Irwin 1978). The orientation of temples on the cardinal compass points refers to the establishment of order out of the void – to stand four-square is to affirm the order of things and one's place in it.

The nailing of the mound can also be seen as referring to the time when man ceased to be nomadic, following the 'earth-spirit' or telluric force in its natural annual wanderings. When he settled and began to farm, it was necessary to pin down this errant, life-nurturing source, to control and direct its flow. So the natural connection between sky and earth was broken; and complex observations and rituals were needed to find the moments when this contact could be re-established.

Festivals and rites

One of the most striking facts about megalithic monuments is their very specific orientation. From the first megaliths onwards, the direction in which their entrances faced seems to have been of importance. The early dolmens in Portugal face south of east, roughly towards the midwinter sunrise, as does that of the even older Kercado chambered mound at Carnac. The English long barrows, later, face east. A thousand years after Kercado was built, the great monument of Newgrange in Ireland was aimed clearly at the winter solstice sunrise — on midwinter day, and on only a day or two either side of it, the rising sun shines straight through a horizontal slit above the entrance to the mound, down the long passage, and illuminates the spiral rock-carvings of the chamber within. Not all chambers of this first thousand years point in that direction, but the orientation is so common that it is hard to resist the conclusion that the midwinter festival was the most important at that stage and the moment of rebirth of the sun the chief focus of veneration. We can imagine, in the chambers and in the forecourts and stone circles around these monuments, ceremonies which witnessed or invoked the sun starting its annual cycle of lengthening days.

Later, the emphasis often seems to switch from the winter to the summer solstice. Stonehenge was rearranged in 2400 BC so that its chief axis lined up with the Heel Stone and the Avenue, towards the midsummer sunrise. The Visbek Bride alignment in Germany also points in this direction. But by that time the megalith builders were also putting up structures which appear to be related to the moon's cycles, quite possibly with the chief objective of predicting and ritualizing eclipses of sun or moon.

The midsummer and midwinter solstice, and the spring and autumn equinox, would form natural divisions of the year into four seasons, each to be marked by a gathering with feasts and ceremonies to mark the event. The eclipses would provide irregular but very special occasions for rites to mark the restoration of the sun or moon's light, the most awe-inspiring natural expression of death and rebirth.

All this shows the importance given to marking a very precise point in the annual cycle (and through the eclipses, in much longer cycles), of synchronizing rituals with the wheeling patterns of the skies. The emphasis on orientation may also reflect a related but slightly different intention – the aligning of the monument on the path along which the awaited force, or deity, is expected to come. As John Michell puts it, 'the sanctity of local shrines extends to the paths that lead up to and between them. The god approaches his shrine by a particular route.' (Michell 1975, 9–10.)

One other type of seasonal festival must be considered. The Celts who occupied much of Europe well after the last megaliths were built in about 1500 B C, celebrated four major annual festivals whose descendants still survive today. It is quite possible that much older holy days are preserved in the Celtic customs. Imbolc was at the start of February, Beltane on May Day or its eve, Lugnasadh at the beginning of August and Samhain at the end of October or start of November. In the same order, we have Candlemas, May Day, Harvest Festival and All Hallows' Eve (or All Saints' Day) in the Christian or secular calendars. Samhain was a fire-festival (though fire was important in other Celtic festivals too). Peasant customs of leaping, or driving farm animals through, burning lines of straw at that season survived into the last century, while in the best folklore style, the very ancient Samhain fires have been cheerfully dedicated to a new hero and continue as Guy Fawkes night. Bonfires still appear in folk rituals in many parts of Europe while the maypole is ubiquitous throughout the Continent. There is no evidence that these festivals are older than Celtic, but large amounts of unexplained ash have been found at megalithic sites in various parts of Europe, quite apart from ash which seems to be associated with cremation or with domestic sites.

The objects of veneration at such ceremonies, and therefore the nature of the most sacred rituals, clearly varied from place to place and occasion to occasion. In general it does not seem that the existence of a cult object at a megalithic site necessarily precluded the celebration of the overriding celestial or terrestrial events in the same monument. Thus the cult of the double-axe in Denmark around 3000 B C and of the bull or the Mother Goddess in the Mediterranean may have been combined with proper attention to the sun at its crucial passages from one season to another. The general picture that emerges seems to be of mankind's concern to keep in harmony with the forces that controlled the wellbeing of the earth and its fertility. Rites for this general purpose can be pictured at the monuments from Newgrange to Bari and from Malaga to

Tustrup. There is plenty of direct evidence of ceremonial libation from shattered pottery and other objects at megalithic sites. One notable example of this has emerged from the painstaking work done at the Grønhøj dolmen in Denmark, sorting through more than seven thousand potsherds. In some places, notably Malta, there are clues pointing to animal sacrifice, but these seem to have been localized practices. There is no evidence of human sacrifice.

The forms of the monuments themselves suggest various kinds of ritual. The avenues, alignments, and outlying stones at Avebury, Stonehenge, Carnac, Wéris and Callanish very powerfully evoke images of great processions, whatever their astronomical or other functions may have been. And the big enclosures and courts are obvious settings for that dance which seems to have been men and women's earliest way of worshipping and celebrating, and of restoring themselves to harmony with the rhythms of life. 'The dance plays a crucial role, as expression of the natural seizure of early man. Originally all ritual was a dance, in which the whole of the corporeal psyche was literally "set in motion"' (Neumann 1955, 298). The way the earth is worn around a barrow at Winterbourne Whitchurch in England and another at Sutton in Wales is suggestive of constant pounding by human feet – this is important too, as suggesting that chambered mounds were for ritual other than burials. There are Mesolithic rock drawings in Sicily showing men dancing around two central figures, and another in Spain shows nine women with skirts dancing around a man – these are earlier than any megaliths. From the Bronze Age rock-drawings, there are dancers at Val Canonica in Italy and men and women circling around a maypole in Scandinavia. A carving found in one of the *nuraghi* in Sardinia, dated before 1000 BC from the last megalithic culture, shows three women in an ecstatic dance around a standing stone (Burl 1976, 85 and 88).

This dance must have been accompanied by music of some sort, but the earliest surviving musical instruments only go back to the early Bronze Age, when the last and most intricate megaliths were built. Pottery drums have been found in Germany, a pan-pipe in Poland, and a pipe carved from a swan's bone in England.

Mankind and nature

Many imaginative theories have been put forward to provide an overall explanation for the megaliths of western Europe. Some see them as the fringe of a great civilization called Atlantis, now disappeared under the ocean. Others believe they are evidence of the intervention of an extra-terrestrial intelligence in our ancestors' affairs, perhaps those who control the unidentified flying objects so often reported. Whatever we make of these ideas and the others summarized in this introduction, there is evidence enough that a remarkable culture – or cultures – flourished in Europe between 5000 and 1500 BC. The traces of that culture seem to show a society which, at least until the coming of metal, was freer of war than the continent has ever been since that time. Even violence seems to have been rare though occasional signs of theft and murder have been found; the early monuments have no defences and no weapons suitable for more than hunting. Mankind seems to have been concerned with achieving and maintaining a harmonious relationship with nature, with farming and hunting for food, with erecting great monuments as their spiritual and festival centres and with studying the complex workings of the universe.

1   Carnac and the Great Menhir

Carnac, on the south coast of Brittany, is the greatest centre of megaliths in the world. From a few centuries after 5000 BC until some time after 2000 BC, men of the Neolithic and early Bronze Ages of western Europe built a series of increasingly complex structures: the dolmens, which some archaeologists think were only the stone chambers of graves deep under earth mounds; menhirs, the lovely tall stones standing in solitude; giant cairns and man-made mounds; and the great multiple alignments of standing stones which run for kilometres across the gently undulating and often wooded countryside. For centuries people have wondered at these great granite monuments, and argued about who built them, and how, and for what extraordinary purpose?

The earliest date we have yet for a megalithic monument is for the large Kercado stone chamber and mound on one of the highest hills in the district, south-east of the Kermario alignment. Organic material from burials here has been radiocarbon tested during the last few years and has shown that Kercado was in use in 4700 BC – a date well before the palace phases of Knossos in Crete. It is an impressive place to visit The chamber and its mound are quite well preserved; around the mound, a circle of standing stones can still be seen among the pine trees and another upright stone stands on the very peak of the mound. The entrance of the megalithic chamber faces thirty-two degrees south of east, almost exactly towards the midwinter sunrise. The significance of this orientation of the passage has been discussed in the introduction.

It may be that the small town of Carnac is one of the oldest continuously inhabited places in the world. The vast number of megalithic monuments in the area seems to show Carnac as a comparatively densely populated centre of Neolithic culture, yet only a few groups of contemporary dwellings – such as the village remains at Le Lizo above the nearby Crach river – have been found. Such a scarcity of dwellings is usual at other megalithic sites, but one explanation put forward by

1. The Kercado chambered mound on a hilltop near Carnac, Brittany. The mound is surrounded by a circle of standing stones and there is a single menhir, which can be seen here, on its peak. Its calibrated radiocarbon date of 4700 BC is the earliest for a megalithic monument yet discovered anywhere.

archaeologists is that the Neolithic habitations lay where the houses of modern Carnac lie today, a mile inland from the present coastline. On the north-east edge of the town rises a man-made mound, rather like Avebury's Silbury Hill in its central position and its relationship to the many monuments in the surrounding countryside. This hill is now known as the Tumulus St Michel. Its height of nearly 40 feet (12 metres) is small compared with Silbury's 130 feet (40 metres), but the Tumulus is just as dominant a presence in the lower hills of the Carnac

2. The man-made mound at Carnac, now called the Tumulus Saint Michel. Radiocarbon dates from material found in small stone chambers inside the mound go back to around the same period as Kercado, but the date of the sacred mound itself is not established. It has the half-pear form often found in hills shaped by men.

countryside and it is far older. Radiocarbon datings for the innermost stage of Silbury show a date of 2600 BC, while the series of small graves in the Carnac hill go back beyond 4000 BC and the mound itself may well be much earlier.

Archaeologists have asserted that the purpose of both these great hills was to cover a grave, but repeated excavations at Silbury have failed to find a burial chamber. At the Tumulus St Michel, Zacharie le Rouzic's work in 1906 revealed a series of small dolmen-type chambers and cists, some holding human remains with grave goods, others containing animal bones. He made a narrow twisting tunnel through the hill from one

Fig. 7. Carnac, the great menhir Er Grah, and some of the major megaliths in the area. Professor Thom has shown that Er Grah could have been used as a universal lunar foresight for observations from various positions around it (see Fig. 3).

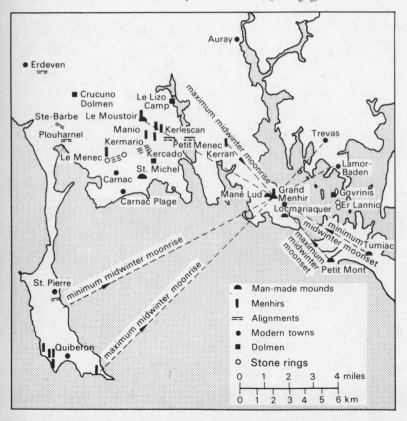

chamber to another which one can still follow today. The idea that these little tombs could be the main reason for building this tremendous mound seems totally unconvincing.

Christianity has always been quick to take over the sacred places of older cults, and when the new religion arrived at Carnac its priests must have seen the need to claim the most important holy site. There are other man-made mounds in the region about the same size as the Tumulus St Michel, notably the Mané-er-Hroeck chambered cairn six miles to the east, but it was the Carnac hill that was renamed after St Michael the dragon slayer and then capped by a Christian chapel. Its overall shape, rounded at its broader end and narrowing to a point like a pear, is similar to that of many other sacred hills in northern Europe.

3. The stone ring or cromlech at Le Menec, where the series of great alignments starts at Carnac. The stones are about four feet high. The ring cuts through part of a hamlet. It probably dates from the same period as the alignments, perhaps between 2500 and 2000 B C.

The function of the great artificial hills associated with late Stone Age men will never be discovered by scientific archaeology alone. To come to understand them we may have to imagine a religion which saw the natural forces of the earth and the skies, the passage of the seasons, the shape of the landscape, and the relationship between them, as intimately embodying spiritual truths; manifesting at the same time the order of the cosmos and the means for human beings to bring themselves into harmony with it. The importance given to celestial observation was one expression of this religion; another was the common siting of major megalithic monuments in a special configuration of hills and lowlands, as we described in the introduction to this book. We see these great man-made hills (without major tomb-chambers inside) as sacred centres where the great forces of earth and sky were gathered, at least symbolically, and from which, at the right season, they would energize the soil again, and make it fruitful.

Half a mile north of the town of Carnac the three famous alignments begin at the little hamlet of Le Menec. Many of the houses lie actually within the remains of a ring of standing stones – known in France as a 'cromlech' – at the western end of the alignment. The cromlech cuts right through the hamlet, its row of flat upright slabs, about four feet high, continuing shoulder to shoulder except where interrupted by houses or lanes. It is by no means a pure circle but has the overall egg-shape familiar from many British sites. Nor is the ring central to the eleven rows of big standing stones or menhirs which run off in an east-north-east direction to another remnant of a cromlech in a wood 1200 yards away. Like all the Carnac alignments, the stones of Le Menec start tall (some more than 12 feet or 3.6 metres high) and the avenues between the rows are broad. As one walks towards the east, the average height of the stones diminishes steadily and the avenues narrow. After passing a gap where farmers have cleared away the stones for agriculture, one finds that the end of the alignment includes many stones only knee-high and the avenues are less than half their original width. The impression is that the alignments are gigantic arrowheads pointing to the east from the west or, alternatively, spreading fans rising towards the sky for an observer from the east. Many megalithic monuments in other countries of Europe are aligned in this general direction – west to east, or south-west to north-east – and we shall be speculating later in the book about the purpose of these structures.

A few hundred metres farther east the most impressive group of all begins, the Kermario alignment. There was probably a western stone

4. Part of Le Menec alignment, the first of the three multiple rows at Carnac.

ring here, too, but it has disappeared and only a fine dolmen has escaped the car-park which has covered the site.

Ten alignments of standing stones as tall as 18 feet (5.5 metres) run down into a shallow valley beside a farmhouse, then, decreasing in size, up the farther slope and past the stump of an old windmill tower. Beyond the tower the smaller lines of stones continue as the land drops again – they cross a burial mound, presumably older, turn very slightly to the north and go through what is now a pond before ending in thick woods.

Again, the length of the alignment is over a thousand metres to the final small surviving stones. But it is among the tall boulders of the western start of Kermario that one senses most strongly the magical power of the Carnac stones. As mentioned in the introduction, dowsers record very marked 'currents' from many megalithic structures. These

5. The Kermario alignment, perhaps the most impressive of all the three long rows of standing stones.

often form concentrated 'bands' of force at regular intervals above and below ground level – some dowsers have been quite literally flung to the ground by the strength of the force at the fifth level. But many of us who are (perhaps luckily) less sensitive, can still learn to sense these currents with the palm of the hand – some people feel it as a tingling or prickling, others as a warmth, or just as a slight change of temperature. Just what these forces may be, whether the stone-builders could manipulate or use them in some way – and if so, how – are for us some of the most fascinating questions raised by the megaliths, wherever one sees them. In some sites the stones seem quite neutral, almost 'dead', in others we get a sense of great energy lying somehow dormant. Still others seem very highly charged. Here that sensation is at its strongest, especially at a great menhir which stands at right angles to the lines in the middle of one of the central avenues. It is a massive stone which

6. The 20 feet (6.2 metres) high menhir at the sanctuary of Le Manio, near the easterly end of the Kermario alignment. This singularly beautiful stone may have acted as an astronomical foresight from several distant positions, as shown in the diagram in the introduction.

must have been crucially important to the ritual and purpose of this place. To visit these alignments and move around the big rocks in daylight is memorable. On a moonlit night it is awe-inspiring.

The third Carnac alignment, Kerlescan, starts a quarter of a mile beyond the eastern end of the Kermario lines, but there are two other notable megaliths near this point. A little way to the south along an entrance drive to a château lies Kercado, the very ancient passage grave and barrow of 4700 B C already mentioned (the key can be obtained from the château).

To the north, up a lane through the pine trees, there is another place with its own sacred atmosphere. In a clearing in the woods stand the Manio enclosure and the great Manio menhir. The enclosure, almost an oblong, is an uneven quadrilateral of fairly low standing stone slabs, with one end of this trapezoidal plan divided off into a small forecourt by another line of stones. The usual explanation of this enclosure is that the stones were a kerbing for a mound containing a grave, both of which have now disappeared. Equally, on the available evidence, it may have provided some other type of sanctuary. At right angles to the east end of the enclosure, and a few metres away, stands the magnificent Manio menhir; 20 slender feet of smoothly rounded stone rising among the pine trees. Moving in its beauty and presence, this stone is one of the largest in the Carnac area. It is one of four outlying menhirs to the north of the Carnac alignments which Professor Thom has suggested may have been the backsights and foresight of an observatory for sun and moon settings, before the growth of the pine woods obscured the sight-lines between them.

The third of the Carnac alignments, Kerlescan, starts a little way to the east of the Manio menhir. What remains of Kerlescan today is much shorter than the other two famous alignments. The lines start from a very big and almost square cromlech or enclosure of tall standing stones, like an open court for human gatherings. The western menhirs of the thirteen lines are large and bulky, but less tall than in the other two alignments. They reduce in size more quickly, and the avenues narrow more rapidly, too, and they point almost due east. At the end of the Kerlescan lines there are farmhouses and then a road. Across the fields beyond the road there is another alignment which takes a sudden bend towards the north. This alignment – also known as Petit Menec – may originally have been a continuation of Kerlescan, or it may have been separate. The farthest stones of Petit Menec, after a sudden northward bend in the lines, finish beside a minor road and are rarely visited.

7. The Kerlescan alignment at Carnac, the last of the series of three which together run approximately east-north-east for several kilometres.

We end the long course of the Carnac alignments with a feeling of awe at the grandeur of these structures, and the mystery of their purpose. Were they processional routes for rituals that marked and responded to the passage of the seasons? Were they paths to draw fertile energies of earth and sky together into the soil of Carnac? Certainly they must have been seen as centrally important to the communities that built them, over a span of many centuries. And this sense of their importance seems to have survived until modern times, for the Abbé Mahé, writing in 1825, records a verbal tradition that the alignments were added to each year, in June. On the eve of the set day, all the stones were illuminated, at great expense to the people. And Cambry, in 1805, writes of 'This stone offered to the stars each year. . . .' He continues: 'This stone . . . reminds me of the Nails of the Capitol, and of the Etruscans, which marked the years for these people before they adopted writing in their religious ceremonies.' Then, trying to find the hidden sense of this practice, he goes on, 'The stars resemble nailheads stuck into the vault of heaven; to place a new nail in the temple of Jupiter in times of plague, of extraordinary and terrifying events, was to put oneself under the protection of a new star, a new God.'

Only one modern man has made a scientifically convincing statement to explain at least part of the purpose of the Carnac alignments – the former professor of engineering at Oxford University, Alexander Thom. Professor Thom, after many years of work on megaliths in Britain, came to Carnac in 1970 and for the following five years and has now carried out the first really accurate surveys of its best-known standing stones. Thom's theory, well demonstrated, is that the alignments were refined instruments for foretelling eclipses (Thom 1971, Feb. 1972, Oct. 1972, 1973 and 1974). The movements of the moon as observed from earth are extremely complex. As was outlined in the introduction in the section on astronomy, to foretell an eclipse it is necessary to measure the position of the moon at maximum declination – which may occur at a time when it cannot be seen from a particular place on earth. By using parts of the alignments like a great piece of graph paper, the position of the moon at moonset for several successive nights could be plotted by stakes, and the resulting curve could be continued to show the positions when the moon was out of sight and to reveal the time of maximum declination. These lines would be plotted on the alignments from the observations of the moon (and perhaps the sun in other cases) made with the aid of the outlying menhirs, most notably the Manio Menhir and the Great Menhir at Locmariaquer.

The Great Menhir lies some six miles east of the Tumulus St Michel and the town of Carnac. In the year 1659 a French naval officer sent a report about a wrecked ship to the Admiralty in Paris, mentioning that the great stone of 'Locmariaker' could be seen from the place where the ship was lost. Er Grah, the Great Menhir, must surely be the stone which he meant. Today it lies shattered on the ground in four huge pieces, several hundred metres from the nearest water, and a drawing dated 1727 shows it in that state. Unless that naval lieutenant made some extraordinary mistake, the highest of all megalithic standing stones had been smashed by lightning, earth tremor or some other force during the years between.

8. Er Grah or Le Grand Menhir Brisé (the great broken menhir), which now lies in four big pieces in a meadow outside Locmariaquer, a few kilometres east of Carnac. Originally it was more than 60 feet (18.5 metres) high and is thought to have been erected here around 2000 BC as a huge foresight which could be used for astronomical observations from positions far away. The ends of the broken pieces show the shape typical of Breton menhirs.

The Great Menhir was over 60 feet (18 metres) high, three times the height of the largest menhirs usually found and almost twice as high as the next tallest, that of Plouarzel. And it was much more than just the tallest of the megaliths. According to Professor Thom's researches, it stood at the centre of a vast lunar laboratory spread across the land and seascape around Carnac, the ultimate achievement of long centuries of astronomical experiments. Observers from backsight menhirs as much as nine miles away could use the Great Menhir as a foresight for checking the rising or setting moon's position. Variations in the observers' findings could then be examined and forecasts of eclipses could be extrapolated by calculations using the Carnac alignments. There may be a dim echo of lost understanding of this in the folk tale attached to the Menhir des Louérs at St Aubin des Châteaux. There is said to be a clock within the stone, 'and if you put your ear to the stone you will hear the hours strike'.

Many attempts have been made to estimate the date when these alignments and the major menhirs around them were erected (Le Rouzic 1901 to 1939, revised Jacq). Standing stones rarely provide datable archaeological evidence such as that found in graves, and scholars have put forward dates ranging from 4000 to 2000 BC. Certainly the Carnac alignments were built later than some of the mounds and dolmens in the area, for it has been mentioned that the Kermario alignment runs right over one of these. A date of around 2500 to 2000 BC then seems likely from what is known of the dates of other sophisticated megalithic observatories elsewhere.

Alexander Thom has gone a long way towards unravelling the purpose of the Great Menhir and of the Carnac alignments. His theories imply a high degree of social and scientific development in the Neolithic builders. For instance he has calculated that it would have required accurate observations and record-keeping for a period of more than a hundred years to begin to plot this giant observatory. Just how does a pre-literate society gather and preserve this kind of information? As an engineer, Professor Thom is particularly well-qualified to appreciate the social and technological organization that would be needed to build these structures. Theories which seem simple, obvious and satisfying to an archaeologist may look altogether more daunting to a civil engineer. So Thom's answers in turn raise many new questions, and leave us with many other mysteries unsolved. The whole length of the alignments could not be used as he suggests – they certainly had other functions too. Two miles north-west of Carnac there starts a series of four or more smaller alignments at intervals along a straight road running for about seven miles north-north-west from Plouharnel to St-Barbe, Erdeven and St-Cado. The alignments of standing stones at these villages do not point in the direction of this road, but across it, with an orientation which is east–west or near it.

The Erdeven alignment is of particular note because of a sanctuary of four tremendous menhirs, enclosed by tall hedges, just north of the stone rows. This group of menhirs is arranged in a diamond pattern, although two of them have fallen, and the sanctuary has a brooding peace that is exceptional even in the Carnac area. On the other side of the hedge, life bustles on; children running down a footpath; a farmer and his wife working in the field; beyond them cars passing on the road; but sitting here, feeling the deeply worn hollows, wondering if they were made by water, or by man ('That's where the blood used to flow down!' said the farmer, visiting us later), here everything is still and tranquil.

The north-north-west compass line near which these alignments are positioned may possibly have some significance for a celestial observatory, but there are other orientations which surely do not. The Great Menhir, Er Grah, originally stood at one end of a long mound which ran due north–south, while the mound of the notable long barrow at Kerlescan – north of the alignment of the same name – is oriented due east–west. Megalithic structures which point roughly north-east are often directed towards the midsummer sunrise, as we shall see in other parts of Europe. Such an orientation can be achieved by simple observation. But monuments which are aligned towards the cardinal points of the compass imply a different kind of knowledge and symbolism. They recall W. R. Lethaby's comment in 1891 about the fact that most temples all over the world are found to be four-squarely sited with their sides north, south, east and west – 'This four squareness was a talismanic assurance of permanence and stability.' Examples of cardinal orientation occur in major megaliths from Denmark to the Mediterranean, as well as in Brittany.

The country around Carnac is thick with dolmens, cairns and menhirs of widely varying forms. Many more questions come to mind as one looks at them. For example, the so-called passage graves such as Kercado or the Table des Marchands beside the Great Menhir – mounds with a passage leading to a single or multiple chamber – occur only near the coast. On the other hand, the gallery graves of the Plouharnel

9. The Crucuno dolmen, in the countryside north of Carnac, is perhaps the most spectacular of many large dolmens in the area.

type – long rectangular chambers, often with a forecourt before the main structure – are found all over France, even far inland. Were they made by different peoples? And then one becomes aware that there are a number of typical shapes for solitary menhirs and for standing stones in the alignments. Particular slender forms or broadly massive ones, pears standing on their pointed ends or rotund shapes with a slimmer twisted top-knot – these and others recur time and again at Carnac and elsewhere. Were these differing forms symbolical only, or did they have some specific function?

The Great Menhir itself was apparently a typical single menhir shape on a vast scale, tall and slender with flattened sides and a smoothly rounded tip. Apart from its size and its astronomical importance, it is remarkable in another way. The nearest known quarry for the quartzite granite of which Er Grah is made occurs fifty miles away in Finistère.

Yet the menhir must have weighed about 340 tons. It has been suggested that it came from the west side of the Quiberon Peninsula, where there may have been an outcrop now submerged by the altered sea-level. If not, we have a transport task immensely greater than that involved in getting the Bluestones to Stonehenge from Wales. Even from Quiberon, the engineering problem of moving the Great Menhir was a triumph for Neolithic men to overcome. The archaeological finds at Carnac do not include any weapons suitable for making war, so perhaps here those human energies were directed into very different achievements.

Another question often raised is the old one of whether all 'dolmen' type megaliths were originally tombs. Standing up inside a stone structure such as the famous Crucuno dolmen three miles north-west of Carnac, we wonder whether it was really earth-covered and think of Glyn Daniel's words about the Loire megaliths; 'If we believe, as seems to me inevitable that many . . . were never covered with barrows, we are forced to think again about their purpose, and the only non-sepulchral suggestion we can make for these large and impressive structures is that they are some kind of religious monuments.' In any case, the use of a megalithic monument for burials is perfectly compatible with its use for other purposes. Here we would like to mention the account by Le Scouëzec (1976) of the Breton 'enclos paroissial' which may throw some light on this question. This institution occurs throughout Brittany, and not in the rest of France, though it has similarities to the English churchyard. This 'parish enclosure' is a consecrated area at the centre of the town or village. It is the place where the people meet each Sunday, reaffirming their sense of community. And this is not confined to the living, for held close in that sacred space, the dead too are included. (This sense of a common world shared by the living and the dead is shown in old stories of the Celts accepting promises payable in the next life for debts incurred in this one.) The typical enclosure consists of a low stone wall encircling the cemetery, the church, the ossuary, and the Calvary. Into the wall is set the main entrance, often a handsome gateway; other paths in are barred by upright stone slabs which have to be stepped over.

The church usually stands in the middle of the *enclos paroissial,* so that one can walk all round it without leaving the consecrated ground. The ossuary may be freestanding, or backed onto the outer wall, or it may be built out from the choir of the church. These ossuaries held the remains of the dead once the flesh, etc had been removed by the process of time and earth; they were in use till the end of the nineteenth century. The Calvary often stands by the path leading to the main door of the church – outside the churchyard they are found at crossroads. Brittany is richer in these crosses and Calvaries than any other part of France; the first crosses were rudely carved on to existing menhirs, and gradually evolved into the elaborate, even fantastic, Calvary which reached its height in the sixteenth century.

We see this as possible evidence of a long unbroken tradition of an enclosure dedicated to the common life of the people, marked out by a low stone wall or kerb; a meeting-place closely associated with the centre of their religious rites. Here the living put the remains of the dead for safekeeping, and in turn the dead watched over the heart of the community. These sacred places and the paths to them were marked and guarded by standing stones.

Two more remarkable megalithic structures lie beyond the Great Menhir from Carnac. On two islands in the Golfe du Morbihan are Er-Lannic and Gavr'inis. In Neolithic times the Golfe was dry land. The intersecting rings of standing stones at Er-Lannic would at that time have stood on a fairly steep slope. This in itself is an extremely unusual siting for stone rings (although it does call to mind the twin siting of the Maltese temples) but today the place is quite extraordinary. The

10. Gavr'inis, in the Golfe du Morbihan, east of Carnac. The mound above the famous carved chamber can be seen on top of the island.

lower ring is completely submerged by the sea, while the stones of the higher circle seem to be stepping down the side of the island and into the water. Archaeological finds around the circles point to a date of about 2500 BC – these finds included traces of huts, domestic debris, pottery and hearths with much charcoal in them (Burl 1976, 134). One of the standing stones has cupmarks roughly in the pattern of the Great Bear constellation – different stars of this constellation are said to have been usable as near-Pole Stars until about 3000 BC.

Gavr'inis, on the island immediately to the north, is a very different monument. On top of the island, as one approaches in the motor boat from Lamor-Baden, a large cairn can be seen. The Carnac area has many dolmens with mysterious Neolithic motifs carved on the stones – those in Les Pierres Plates at Locmariaquer are good examples. But Gavr'inis is quite simply the finest decorated passage grave of all, with Newgrange in Ireland as its only possible rival. Twenty-three of the twenty-nine great slabs which form the walls of Gavr'inis are carved with intricate spirals, intersecting multiple semicircles, and other whorled patterns. It is not yet known whether these patterns are purely decorative or whether they have some religious significance. A meaning or a symbolism seems likely, since the spiral forms occur so often in Neolithic carving, but the code remains hidden.

11. Er Lannic, another island in the Golfe du Morbihan. The standing stones of one ring, dating from about 2500 BC, can be seen running down into the edge of the water. The other stone ring has been submerged since the sea engulfed the valley.

12. Detail of one of the many intricately carved stones in the Gavr'inis chamber. The carved chamber is thought to be roughly contemporary with that of Newgrange in Ireland, which is well before 3000 B.C.

The stone structures described here are the chief glories of the Carnac area. There are many more, and weeks could be spent wandering happily in search of other great monuments in the countryside with the help of the guidebooks available locally. Here we are going on to describe many of the other major megalithic sites in western Europe, but again and again we shall find ourselves referring back to this, the richest of all centres of the megalith builders.

2 The Rest of France and Italy

The fame of the Carnac megaliths in Brittany has quite overshadowed the fact that all except the eastern side of France is rich in Neolithic monuments scarcely less imposing. The map based on the French survey published in 1956–7 shows the distribution of nearly 4500 megaliths of all sizes, making clear their prevalence along the west coast and across the comparatively narrow neck of France between the Bay of Biscay and the Mediterranean Sea. From the French Riviera to the

Fig. 8. Outline map of France showing the distribution of megalithic monuments, based on the survey published in 1956–7. The density around the north-westerly coasts and across the neck of land to the Mediterranean is very marked.

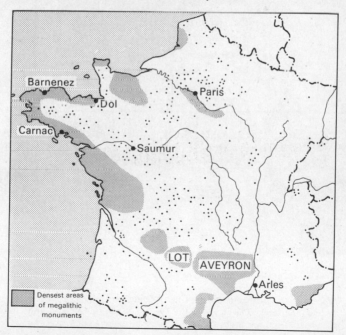

13. The broader face of the Menhir du Champ Dolent at Dol, on the borders of Brittany and Normandy. This is one of the largest surviving menhirs, over 30 feet (9.50 metres) in height, and was probably erected at about the same time as Er Grah.

east around the Mediterranean there is then a large gap where no megaliths have been found, extending from Piedmont down to the area around Naples, where the southern Italian groups begin.

It is known from archaeological finds that Neolithic people had become settled farmers in southern France long before the earliest dates for megaliths occur around 4500 BC, but so far it is not known when such settled cultivation started in Brittany, where those early structures appeared. Certainly, on the basis of present knowledge, the southern French megaliths were not built before about 4000 BC.

Four areas of French megaliths, apart from Carnac, deserve particular notice. The first of these is the rest of Brittany, where the stone structures can be found from end to end of the old duchy and date from the earliest period until the end of the megalithic era. On the north-west coast the huge stepped cairn of Barnenez South, dating from 4500 BC, contains a row of eleven passages running into rounded chambers of almost all types (see frontispiece). There are dolmens and earth-covered passage graves throughout Brittany, as well as alignments of standing stones (probably dating from 2500 to 2000 BC) on a scale dwarfed only by the three largest Carnac rows. Giant single menhirs are also widespread, of which the 30-feet (9.1-metres) Dol menhir, on the borders of Normandy, is one of the finest. These solitary beauties have the shape, broad in one direction but flattened and narrow in the other, of most astronomical standing stones. It may well be that, like the broken Er Grah at Carnac, they were foresights for local observatories. Equally, their scattered positions across large areas of Europe (for tall single standing stones occur in whole regions of Germany, Britain, Belgium, Corsica and other countries too) may mark a prehistoric belief in some network of paraphysical earth energies like the ley lines mentioned in the introduction to this book. Their dates remain mysterious and are likely to remain so unless radiocarbon datable material is found under them.

The second group of French megaliths which need a special mention in this chapter are the huge dolmens, which could be described as temple-dolmens, around Saumur on the river Loire. These are among the most impressive achievements of megalithic architecture anywhere and set archaeologists a special puzzle in that they were apparently never covered with earth.

North of the Loire around Saumur these giant dolmens can be found at Soucelles, at La Roche Thibault (near Jarze), at Baugé, and near Mettray close to Tours (La Grotte des Fées at St Antoine du Rocher).

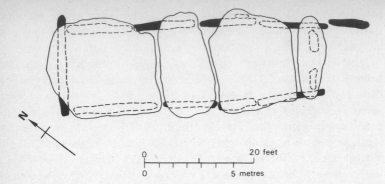

Fig. 9. Plan of Le Grand Dolmen, probably the largest ever built, at Bagneux, a suburb of Saumur on the river Loire. This is one of the Loire group which can probably best be described as temple-dolmens, for they do not appear to have been covered with earth mounds and may never have contained burials.

South of the river in the Saumur region there are more west of Gennes (the Dolmen de la Madeleine), another in a farmyard near St Hilaire (the Dolmen de la Pierre Boire), then the massive Le Gros-Chillou at Briançon, Cravant, which is 50 feet (15.2 metres) long and 10 feet (3.1 metres) high. La Pierre Folle at Bournand is even longer and up to 18 feet (5.5 metres) wide; until recently it was used as a henhouse for the adjoining farm.

The largest of all, and probably the largest capstoned dolmen ever built, is the Grand Dolmen at Bagneux, a suburb of Saumur. The orthostats of this great monument form solid walls, with an entrance facing approximately south-east at one end, and it is covered by four gigantic capstones. The plan is almost rectangular, more than 60 feet (18.3 metres) long and 20 feet (6.1 metres) wide. The chamber is 10 feet (3.1 metres) high, the largest capstone 25 feet (7.6 metres) long and estimated to weigh 86 tons.

The Loire dolmens are similar in plan to the dolmens around Paris itself. But the Paris group had mounds and contained human remains – they were built in trenches and were subdivided internally by stone slabs. In all these respects they differ from the huge Loire monuments. Of those described above and other big dolmens in the Saumur area, only that at St Antoine du Rocher has even the slightest trace of earthworks around it. Moreover, none of them has produced remains of human burials. These facts have driven Glyn Daniel to conclude that they were never in barrows (Daniel 1960, 117) and to write: 'I wonder whether here in the Loire valley and in eastern Brittany . . . what started as a tomb became a temple?' Certainly, anyone approaching and entering the Grand Dolmen will receive the impression much more of an imposing ceremonial interior than of a tomb. The dates of the big Loire dolmens have not yet been established – on the basis of radio-carbon dates for large dolmens elsewhere, an estimate of before 3000 BC seems likely.

Moving farther south, we turn next to the remarkably dense cluster of megaliths in the departments of Aveyron and Lot, in the neck of France between the Dordogne and Languedoc – Biscay and the Mediterranean. There are more megalithic chambered mounds here than in the whole of England and Wales. Of all European megaliths, they are among the farthest from the sea and among the highest above sea-level. Here, there are many stone chambers of the local Jurassic limestone in long barrows strikingly similar to those of southern Britain and Brittany. Even more extraordinary are the dolmens on top of natural hillocks and surrounded by rings of standing stone slabs. General datings for these structures do not appear to have been published.

Last of all, on the French mainland, we shall describe the group of long rock-cut chambers around the great Grotte des Fées near Sainte Croix, about four kilometres along the road north-east from Arles towards the small town of Fontvieille. This group of man-made caverns is tantalizingly elusive, for although one can see the Montagne de Cordes – the hill in which the Grotte des Fées itself is cut – from the ruined Abbaye de Montmajour at the roadside, it is difficult to find the way to it. It is worth stopping at the Abbaye anyway, for a little way along the road on the far side of a manor house stands an outlying chapel. The approach is down some very broad shallow steps, on either side of which are curious coffin-shaped depressions cut into the solid rock.

The Montagne de Cordes is an extraordinary hill in itself, only 65 metres high but of roughly that half pear-shape characteristic of many sacred hills, both natural and man-made, found elsewhere in France and England. The Montagne is thought to have been the highest of three islands which stood above the water of the Rhône estuary in about 3500 BC, when the rock-cut chambers or tombs were made (Hawkes 1977, 54). Today it rises from surrounding flat countryside with the Grotte about two-thirds of the way up its flank on the side facing the main road. The minor road approaching it leaves the highway farther to the east, but the chances of seeing the great chamber are small. The owner of the land keeps the hill as a wildlife sanctuary and warns off

14. The Montagne de Cordes, rising from a flat plain a few kilometres east of Arles in southern France. The great rock-carved chamber known as the Grotte des Fées lies near the upper cliffs to the right of centre in this picture. It is thought to date from between 4000 and 3500 B C.

visitors, while trespassers are met by solid banks of brambles towering overhead and miniature cliffs along the side of the Montagne.

In one way it is regrettable that the Grotte des Fées is not more accessible to visitors, for it is a remarkable monument. Approached from the surface by steps which descend about 11 feet (3.4 metres) into the ground, a long tunnelled ante-chamber – with a lobed cell on either side – leads straight ahead into a slightly tapering main chamber (trapezoidal in section) which is about 80 feet (24 metres) long. Its width is only 9 feet (2.7 metres), but its walls are over 11 feet high (3.4 metres) and are roofed by the solid bedrock which is in turn covered with earth.

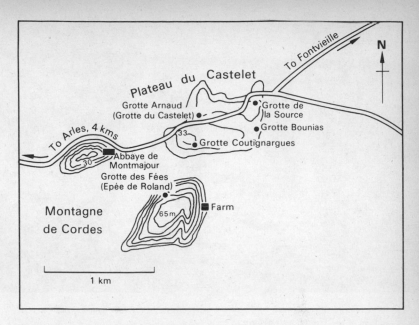

Fig. 10. Outline map showing the rock-cut chambers in the country around the Grotte des Fées, near Arles. Their overgrown entrances into the ground make them extremely difficult to find.

From its plan, the chamber is sometimes known as L'Epée de Roland – though this name may also spring from a sense of the powerful importance of the site.

The lesser rock-cut chambers of the group are easier to reach as long as one can find local help to act as a guide – for although they lie around the main road on another small hill nearby called the Plateau de Castelet, one can be within a few metres of their overgrown entrances without seeing them. The Grotte Arnaud-Castelet lies very close to the north side of the main road in a small oval man-made mound. Here, there is an entrance ramp down to a capstone-covered chamber – again trapezoidal in section – 60 feet (18 metres) long and 7 feet (2.1 metres) wide. The other known chambers – the Grotte Bounias, the Grotte de la Source and the above-ground Dolmen de Coutignargues – lie in the thick scrub of the low hill to the south of the road.

These rock-cut monuments are imposing and enigmatic. Their smoothly worked masonry and elegant proportions speak of cultivated builders and a strong purpose. The Grotte des Fées has been known

15. The interior of the Grotte de Castellet-Arnaud, one of the four smaller rock-cut chambers of the Grotte des Fées group near Arles.

Fig. 11. Plan and sections of the Grotte des Fées on the Montagne de Cordes, near Arles in southern France. The chamber is thought to have been cut around 3500 BC.

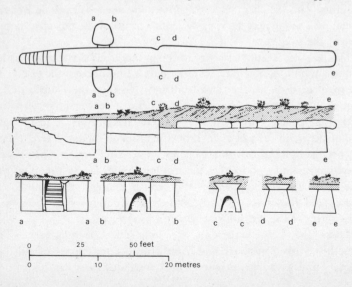

for centuries and it has not been excavated – today it is as if it were being guarded from profanation. The Grotte Arnaud-Castelet has been excavated and, despite its use as a forge for nearly 400 years, the remains of over 100 skeletons were found, as well as axes, arrowheads and manufactured articles of bone, callaïs, steatite, shell, pottery both early undecorated and later Beaker type, and gold. The other Plateau de Castelet chambers produced similar human remains and objects, as well as a bead of copper and a pendant of rock-crystal. The Grotte de la Source has a serpentine line ending in a wheel surrounded by cupmarks on the upper surface of a capstone, now hidden by earth. On the rocks around the chambers have been found other carvings – these have been interpreted as sun-symbols and hint at the non-funerary rites performed there. It would appear that the tombs were used from the date of their construction in perhaps 3500 BC until Beaker People times, possibly as late as 2000 BC. Rock-cut chambers are found in other parts of southern France – although the Arles group is the most magnificent there – in northern France on the Marne river, in Sardinia, in Sicily, in Malta and elsewhere in the Mediterranean.

South-east of Provence we find a large part of Europe where no signs of megaliths have been found. The reasons for this gap of hundreds of kilometres of coastline are obscure. Except in southern Spain, Corsica and Sicily the megalith builders seem to have avoided savagely mountainous sites, so it is not surprising that there are none along the steeply Alpine coasts of south-eastern France and north-western Italy. But the rest of the western coast of Italy offers countryside where mountains and their foothills alternate with coastal plains, just as in many areas rich in megaliths. Yet apart from a small group of comparatively minor chamber tombs in the region around Rome and Naples, the only megaliths in mainland Italy are in the heel, right in the south-east.

Three possible explanations come to mind. All the megalithic remains might have been destroyed in what is one of the most intensely built and rebuilt parts of the earth's surface: but this seems extremely unlikely. Secondly, it is just conceivable that prevailing winds and currents kept these seafaring people away: but then how did they get to the heel of Italy? The most likely explanation is that most of Italy was already occupied by formidable people who would have no truck with the megalith builders or who already had a religion flourishing enough to withstand their rituals and building mania.

In Sicily the story is different. The so-called Stentinello culture

16. Italy. The dolmen at Bisceglie, near Bari in the south-east. Thought to date from about 2300 BC, it can be seen here that this is the remains of a long chamber of the gallery grave type, and large enough for a tall man to stand upright inside.

around Syracuse was developed by a Neolithic people from about 4000 BC onwards (Guido 1967, 23). The first metal-workers appeared perhaps a thousand years later, introducing the idea of rock-cut tombs which remained popular with later Sicilian people.

By about 2000 BC, copper gave way to bronze as the chief metal used. The chief known example of this period's quasi-megalithic architecture is the prehistoric village of Castelluccio, inland between Syracuse and Ragusa, and its rock-cut cemetery.

Castelluccio, like Los Millares in southern Spain, sits on a spur with steep cliffs falling around it into the valley below. Into the face of the cliffs more than 200 tombs have been cut. No trace has been found of the human dwellings, but large amounts of pottery and debris were on the site. From the existence of pottery similar to the Middle Helladic period of Greece, archaeologists dated the site at between 1800 and 1400 BC (Guido 1967, 155–6). This seemed convincing at a time when the Tarxien cemetery of Malta was thought to be of the same period, for on the stone slabs filling the doorways of the Castelluccio tombs there are carvings of spirals and other motifs superficially similar to those at Tarxien. Moreover, the overhanging pillared galleries cut out of solid rock, which run in front of some Castelluccio tombs, resemble work in the rock-cut underground Hypogeum of Hal Saflieni in Malta. But the Maltese work (qv) is now known from calibrated radiocarbon dating to be much earlier than previously thought, so the dates of Castelluccio need re-examination. From 1400 BC onwards, rock-cut tombs continued in Sicily but the increasing influence of Mycenae, and Greece in general, can be traced from imported wares. The brief contact with western megalithic design seems to have disappeared.

If Sicily produced no true megalithic monuments, the heel of Italy certainly did. A well-known group of dolmens is scattered widely in the olive groves west of Bari. The largest and most imposing of these, a long structure – with one big capstone – of the type known to archaeologists as gallery graves, stands only a few hundred metres from the Bari to Naples autostrada near a service station named Dolmen. It is built in a slight trench and has the remains of a mound discernible around it. But it is difficult to find the stone chamber on foot from the autostrada and the best approach is from the seaside village of Bisceglie. From there a road runs inland for five kilometres before the dolmen is signposted on the left. Farther inland the same road reaches a hill with a hamlet called Cimadromo, where another track leads to the dolmen called Tavolo dei Paladini two kilometres away. A third is near Albarosa, off the road inland to Ruvo di Puglia, but this is difficult to find. These gallery grave type of dolmens, without a broader chamber at the end of the passage, are now believed to date from before 2000 BC and to show cultural links with the main area of the western European megalith builders.

About fourteen kilometres nearer to Bari than these dolmens, there lies a much more ambitious surviving structure. This is generally known as the Giovinazzo gallery grave or cairn (*specchia*, in Italian) and it is without doubt the most impressive megalithic monument known in mainland Italy. It is quite possible that the Bisceglie dolmens all took approximately this form before their stones were pilfered.

The Giovinazzo cairn is best reached from the seaside town of that

17. The circular forecourt at the entrance to the fine Giovinazzo gallery cairn near Bari. It was built about 2200 BC and was used for collective burial for some 300 years. The forecourt and top of the cairn may well have been used for other ritual ceremonies.

18. Detail of the long gallery inside the Giovinazzo cairn and mound, showing the structure of upright slabs, capstones and one of the subdividing slabs across the chamber.

name by taking the larger of the two minor roads which run inland to Terlizzi. The low cairn, though not signposted, can just be seen about 100 metres away on the right of the road soon after crossing the motorway. It is a long megalithic gallery, trapezoidal in section, and runs through a covering cairn of carefully dressed drystone masonry. This cairn was covered with earth until its recent discovery. The long cairn curves slightly, though still lying approximately north–south, with a fine round forecourt of drystone wall at the southern entrance. The whole length of the cairn is about 90 feet (27 metres), but sadly it stands today broken in two – it was discovered when a farmer drove a bulldozer through the earth mound in an effort to flatten his farmland.

19. The Scusi dolmen in an orchard outside Minervino, near Otranto, almost on the tip of the heel of Italy. There are twelve surviving dolmens in this part of Italy, thought to have been built between 2500 and 1800 BC. In design, they are quite different from the gallery chambers around Bari.

The long gallery within, subdivided by septal slabs, contained the remains of many human skeletons and grave goods including Mycenean I pottery. This shows that it was in use around 1800 BC and radiocarbon datings may well show that the monument itself was built considerably earlier. The round forecourt, originally a wide circular shaft into the mound, gives a hint of rituals that were doubtless performed at the entrance, ceremonies for the living performed close to the resting-place of the dead.

The final group of Italian dolmens lies around the pretty port of Ótranto, right at the tip of the heel of Italy and the end of the Romans' Via Appia. The dolmens here have been dated at around 2000 BC by archaeologists, but without firm evidence (Guido 1972, 155). Standing stones, some nearly 10 feet (3 metres) high, have been recorded in the areas around these dolmens, but these are not easy to find. The best known of the group is the Scusi Dolmen, which can just be glimpsed from the road which runs from the inland village of Minervino di Lecce eastwards towards Ótranto, at about 700 metres from the edge of Minervino, on the right. It stands surrounded by olive and fig trees, with its large pierced capstone supported by one large stone and a number of rough columns formed by stones piled on top of each other.

Another group of three or perhaps more overgrown and partly buried dolmens can be seen by really persistent searchers in a field 200 metres from the deserted farm called Masseria Quattro Mácini, which is reached up a track to the right shortly before a minor road, heading northwards from Minervino, reaches the village of Palmariggi. Lastly, twenty kilometres north-west, Margaret Guido reports (Guido 1972, 156) the Dolmen Gurgulante and the Dolmen Placa near the village called Melendugno.

The Italian dolmens have been described in some detail largely because of their interest as a remote outpost of megalithic architecture. The next sites to be examined, those of Iberia and of Malta – only a few kilometres south of Sicily – are also remote from the major concentrations of megalithic monuments, but they are central to all ideas about the megalith builders.

On the Iberian peninsula, around its coastline and along certain rivers, there are large numbers of megalithic remains. Almost all of them are stone chambers of various kinds and they include the oldest known in Europe outside Brittany. Indeed, some archaeologists believe that the whole megalithic tradition spread out from Iberia (MacKie 1977, 154–62).

Among the widespread megaliths in Iberia, three groups are particularly important. These are the early dolmens (called 'antas' locally) of 4500 BC onwards, on the Guadiana river between Evora and

Fig. 12. Outline map showing the distribution of dolmens and other types of megalithic chambers in Iberia – mainland Spain and Portugal (Derived from Savory).

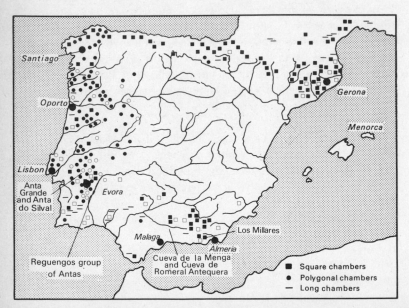

Santiago

Oporto

Gerona

Menorca

Lisbon

Anta Grande and Anta do Silval

Evora

Los Millares

Malaga

Almeria

Reguengos group of Antas

Cueva de la Menga and Cueva de Romeral Antequera

■ Square chambers
● Polygonal chambers
— Long chambers

Mourdo, towards the south of central Portugal: the huge corbelled chambers (or 'cuevas') of perhaps 3500 BC near Malaga in Spain; and the early Copper Age settlement at Los Millares, near Almeria, of around 3000 BC.

The settled farming way of life spread along both coasts of the Mediterranean and reached Spain by 5500 BC, for datable traces of this period have been found near Valencia. These early farmers grew corn and used flint implements. They had a type of pottery, marked with the Cardium seashell, which was common in the eastern Mediterranean. But in Spain they lived in caves around Valencia and in hilltop huts near Almeria, whereas the eastern farmers were living in fortified villages before this time. Some archaeologists believe that the farming culture was spread by word of mouth, perhaps by traders. Others think that an eastern people colonized the coastline, interbreeding with the natives and perhaps with other colonists from Africa. Certainly the human remains from Spain and Portugal of this period show many different ethnic types.

Some of the early people in the Iberian peninsula buried their dead singly in small chambers formed by stone slabs, generally called cists. The first collective burials, in the dolmens which archaeologists call passage graves, are of about 4500 BC. Their age was unknown until recent years, since there are few radiocarbon dates for Spain or Portugal. However, a new dating technique based on the decay of thermoluminescence in pottery is now providing a good deal of information about Iberia.

The group of round chambered mounds on the Guadiana river, east of Evora in Portugal, consists of seven major early tombs with their sides formed by big megalithic slabs up to 5 feet (1.5 metres) high – the roofs seem to have been corbelled with smaller stones, now disappeared, rather than capstones. Goods found in the Anta of Poço da Gateira near the village of Reguengos gave a thermoluminescence date of 4150 BC, with a margin of error of several hundred years either way. These goods included pottery bowls, stone axes and flint blades. The soil is acid and no human bones were found – but the finds were grouped in a way that suggests twelve burials. The nearby Anta dos Gorginos yielded a date of roughly 4440 BC and seems to have had a single burial (MacKie 1977, 33). Only the Kercado monument at Carnac, whose chamber is capstoned and has a standing stone on top of its mound, has provided an earlier date than Poço da Gateira by scientific analysis – and that by a mere two centuries. North and

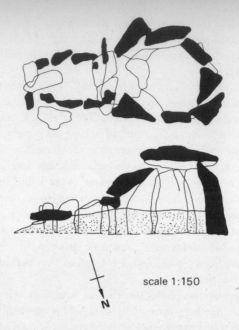

scale 1:150

N

Fig. 13. Plan and section of the Anta do Silval, a large dolmen of the passage grave type, near Evora, Portugal. Portuguese dolmens go back to 4500 BC, but the earliest do not seem to have had capstones.

west of Evora there are other large dolmens and mounds, such as the Anta Grande near Aviz and the Anta do Silval. And around Lisbon itself there are many rock-cut tombs which were built over a period ranging from 4000 to 2000 BC.

Two of the *antas* near the Guadiana river have chambers of a later type right beside them, and this takes us on to the long corbelled tombs of perhaps 3500 BC onwards. They occur in various shapes and sizes in Spain and in Portugal. The most spectacular are the group a few kilometres north of the Spanish port of Malaga, with the immense Cueva de Romeral, and the Cueva de Menga at Antequera as the prime examples of the type (Savory 1968, 110 and 143–8). The Cueva de Romeral has an entrance passage 100 feet (30.5 metres) long into a mound which was originally 30 feet (9.2 metres) high and nearly 300 feet (91 metres) in diameter – very similar to the size of Newgrange in Ireland. The entrance passage is tall and fairly narrow, the drystone walls sloping inwards in a trapezoidal shape to support the capstoned roof

82

(Savory 1968, 143 and 147). Within, there are two magnificent round chambers with corbelled drystone vaulting topped by large capstones. The Cueva de Romeral has not been accurately dated, for it has long been known locally and the archaeologists found little in it. But it remains the grandest architectural achievement of Iberia in the late Neolithic or early Copper Age.

The merging of the late Stone Age with the first use of copper in Spain makes these terms difficult to define. The copper mines were the first worked in western Europe and prospectors were seeking the ore from some time in the fourth millennium BC. The culture which grew up on the prosperity of the copper miners and the making of metal implements is known as Millaran, after the famous site of Los Millares first excavated by the archaeologist Siret early in this century. The copper goods and architectural remains found at Los Millares caused a sensation before the First World War, but little remains to be seen today.

The site of Los Millares lies on a spur high above the Andarax river, about twenty kilometres inland from the port of Almeria in south-east Spain. The main road, and then a smaller road to the left at Benahadux, coil up into arid moon-like mountains. After a stretch passing along the green and fertile Andarax valley, the way rises sharply again into the dry brown hills. Almost immediately, it crosses the Rambla de Huechar (a dry gorge in summer, whose name is signposted on the bridge which spans it) and the site lies unmarked on the spur on the right. The chief impression today is of the threateningly dry and savage mountains around the site. But in 3100 to 2500 BC, when Los Millares flourished, the weather was probably much damper. Here Siret found extensive remains of dwellings, a bastioned wall, outlying forts, a large cemetery and the remains of a major chambered mound surrounded by a circle of standing stones. The chamber in the mound was circular and corbelled, and Siret, linking it with the corbelled tombs of Mycenae, dubbed it misleadingly with the Greek word 'tholos'. It is now known that it is considerably older than the Mycenae tombs. Siret's reconstruction of the circled mound and chamber can be seen in the small but fascinating archaeological museum in Almeria (at present housed in the university buildings). Many of the finds from Los Millares are in this museum too, some of them being mended and restored in the main gallery during our visit. The exhibits provide a much clearer picture of the site than anything remaining on that bleak hillside, where the remains are difficult to pick out from the rocks around them and the

20. The arid landscape of the Andarax valley near Almeria, southern Spain, where the megalithic settlement of Los Millares flourished on a rocky spur above the river between 3100 and 2500 B.C.

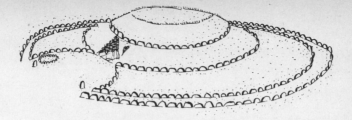

Fig. 14. Reconstruction of a corbelled chambered mound with surrounding stone circles, from the remains found at Los Millares, near Almeria, southern Spain. Believed to date from about 3000 BC.

energies usually associated with megalithic sites seem completely absent.

The Millaran culture spread widely in southern Spain, with many fortifications indicating troubled times quite different from the comparative peace hinted at by most megalithic remains in northern Europe. In Catalonia at the same time, there was a culture which has left many dolmens around Gerona. But after 2500 BC, the older peoples faded and the Beaker culture – which spread throughout western Europe during this millennium – established Bronze Age colonies in Iberia. Whether these people originated from Iberia or spread there from central Europe is a favourite point of dispute for archaeologists. Whatever the truth, much of the vitality of Iberian culture seems to have been lost until after 1000 BC. Apart from a few small stone circles of around 1500 BC reported to exist at Alter Pedroso in the Alentejo, Portugal, and at Medonas da Mourela, Galicia, the building of megaliths does not seem to have developed any further. It is in the Balearics that we find the finest late Spanish megaliths.

4 Malta

The tremendous Neolithic temples of Malta and its neighbouring island Gozo, despite archaeological evidence found recently, remain among the strangest puzzles of all the megaliths. The megalith builders seem simply to have emerged and then, a thousand years later, vanished in the middle of the story of this book.

The earliest Neolithic people probably started farming in Malta around 5000 BC (Trump 1972, 20), judging by calibrated radiocarbon dates from Skorba, the site which gives its name to this earliest period. This is fully as early as the first known Carnac monument date, but the Maltese of that time built nothing notable. By a little after 4000 BC they were building rock-cut tombs, but the temple-building did not start for another 500 years. Then, between about 3500 and 3200 BC, all the great temples were built. Almost all the burials in the tombs associated with the temples are earlier than 3000 BC and by 2500 the whole local civilization was apparently extinct. After a long gap, one temple, Tarxien, was used as a cemetery by Bronze Age people around 2000 BC, and a little later those people or others built a fair number of small dolmens on the Maltese islands. But what happened to the temple builders is unknown.

That earliest settlement, Skorba, in the north of the main island of Malta, is a good but ruined example of a temple of the second magnitude. Like the larger temples, it is one of a pair (Mgarr is nearby) – one in a high commanding position, the other a short distance away, lower down as if cradled by or tucked into the earth. This pairing strikes one very forcibly when looking at the Maltese temples, for it occurs in many connections. As Gertrude Levy has pointed out, there are often pairs of temples sharing a common enclosure; there are pairs of apses and of flanking pillars before the doors; the spiral carvings often occur in pairs; and everywhere there are pairs of the odd double conical cupholes (the holes meet inside the stone – which is why we shall call

Fig. 15. Outline map of Malta and Gozo, showing the megalithic temples and the principal modern cities.

them in-and-out holes). Levy suggests that this duality may possibly embody the cult of a Mother Goddess and young 'Dying' God (Levy 1946). We are drawn to see them as expressing the duality between light, 'sun'-consciousness, and all that is represented by the cave, 'the underworld'. Perhaps one was dedicated to the relationship between earth and sky, the other to the inner body of the earth; or one might have been used for the public, communal rites, the other for more esoteric rites of initiation and transformation.

The Skorba temple's first stages date back to the Ggantija phase of Maltese temples (those with three- or five-lobed apses). The temple

21. Malta. The entrance frontage of the Ggantija south temple, on Gozo. The temple was built in about 3500 BC and, as can be seen in this photograph, towers above human beings.

builders did not start with small-scale structures, however. The big Ggantija temple itself (pronounced roughly Jeguntiya) was built in about 3500 BC. It is at Xaghra in the north of Gozo, the second largest island of the Maltese group. Ggantija is in fact two temples, side by side, both combining truly megalithic bottom stages and doorways with upper layers of a type usually called cyclopean (drystone walling of large pieces of rock). The frontages are concave in plan, as is usual in the Maltese temples. The boulders of the lowest course along the back of Ggantija are particularly gigantic. Within, both have two pairs of lobed chambers opening out of each other. Much can still be seen of the ranges of trilith altars, altar niches, the contemporary cement of the floor, and the worn spiral carvings on one altar. There are holes, perhaps for libations, into the earth and a round hearth before one altar. It

22. Altars in the Ggantija south temple.

is a tremendous work of architectural design and of engineering, built a
thousand years before the date usually given for the Great Pyramid.

The paired temple of Ggantija lies about 300 metres away to the west,
but little can be seen of it today apart from a cave beneath, named Ghar
ta' Chejzu. Both temples stood – at varying heights – looking out over
the fine valley below Xaghra, with a high retaining wall bordering a
broad court in front of Ggantija.

The next pair of temples is in a still more magnificent position. A
visit to the temples of Hagar Qim and Mnajdra (pronounced approximately Hajar Im and Mnaidra), on the south-west coast of Malta itself, is
one of the highest experiences for any lover of megaliths. Hagar Qim is
a temple very much to do with sea and sky, standing on a promontory
which drops away in a hillside towards the Mediterranean. It was built
between about 3500 and 3300 B C. Most of the outer wall consists today of a
single course of giant dressed stones of varying height, with two upper
rows near the lintel of the big trilithon entrance and a low kerb of
stones all round the temple. There were presumably higher courses of
cyclopean structure and then a roof. The material used for the temple
roofs is completely unknown. From a small Neolithic model of a

temple found at Mgarr, it is known that long squared–off beams (rounded at the edges to give an effect like a shallow dome) spanned the whole of each chamber. It is hard to imagine that these were made of anything but big tree-trunks, although Malta today has few sizeable trees. Since a type of cement was used on the floors, it was probably used to seal the roofs too.

Inside, the plan of Hagar Qim is unique, for it is the only one of the Maltese temples enlarged by lobed chambers added to the earliest building, rather than having a second and even a third temple built alongside. The trilithon of the main entrance – which has several 'in-and-out' holes in the stone around it – leads into the usual pair of lobed chambers on either side, and then into a second pair. But here the complexities begin. Instead of another apsed lobe ahead, a second doorway leads out of the back of the temple (near this rear door a single stone of great height projects from the wall in a way that suggests a special purpose). The lobe on the right at this point contains a stone with a porthole in it; on the other side of the porthole is a small chamber, with an external door only, and it has been suggested that ordinary people came there to hear an 'oracle' pronounced by a priest inside. The lobe on the left has no apse wall but was rebuilt to lead past a variety of altars to four other lobed chambers added later. Two of these have doorways to the outside of the temple and, again, their use

23. The frontage, with the main gateway on the right, of Hagar Qim, Malta. The temple was built between 3500 and 3300 BC. The great forecourt, common at the Maltese temples, overlooks the sea on the left.

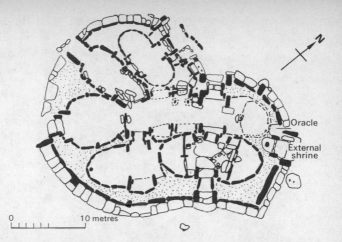

Fig. 16. Plan of the high temple of Hagar Qim, Malta. The lobed chambers on the left-hand side of the plan were apparently added after the temple was first built.

Fig. 16a. Plan of the temples of Mnajdra, down the hill towards the sea from Hagar Qim.

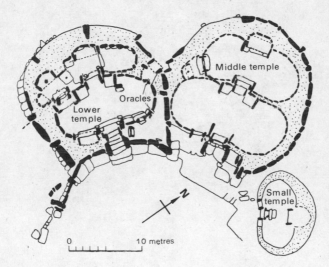

24. The four great rough stones of the Hagar Qim frontage, overlooking the sea and perhaps eroded by its salt.

25. Hagar Qim. Interior of the central aisle which penetrates the site from the main gateway.

by lay-people seems possible. One of the other chambers, doubled back in plan so that it is near the main entrance again, seems an inner sanctum. In it there is a mysterious column altar (of a type usually called a betyl) and an almost hidden miniature chamber; this, one is tempted to think, was the holy place of the Goddess herself, the fertile Goddess with huge belly and thighs, represented in statues, some larger than life, some only a few centimetres high, which have been found here and at other Maltese temples. It is often said that the plan of these temples itself represents the body of the Goddess.

This Great Goddess, the Great Mother, was worshipped at one time or another from India to the Mediterranean, and beyond. As well as her obvious, central role of all-nurturing Earth Mother, she has many other attributes. Erich Neumann tells how as Great Goddess of the Night she is ruler of the unconscious; her priestess is the giver of incubation, the sleep of healing and transformation – 'in the pile dwellings of the Stone Age we already find evidence of the growing of poppies'. In this sleep of incubation, men encounter the healing godhead, they experience oracular dreams. Neumann speaks of this happening 'in Malta long before the days of healing in the Greek shrines of Asclepius'. He draws a parallel, particularly relevant to this book, between the 'slumber of incubation' and being 'drawn through a dolmen, or an ancient stone gate, or in some other way brought to rebirth' (Neumann 1955).

From the edge of the wide platform around Hagar Qim a modern stone path leads down closer to the sea, to the neighbouring temple of Mnajdra. As one walks down the path, the eye is constantly drawn to the small island of Filfla across the water below. The walk takes a few minutes and is memorably beautiful.

Mnajdra does not seem to refer to the sky. The sea is still clearly important to the design, but so is the earth of the hollow in which the building nestles. The similarity of the design to Ggantija is clear as soon as it is seen from its broad forecourt, across which three adjoining temples face the sea.

26. Hagar Qim. One of the lobed areas off the central aisle, with an 'oracle' porthole that pierces the wall into an outer chamber (see plan).

The smallest temple, to the right, is the oldest – it dates from about the same time as Ggantija, and has a simple trefoil plan. Then came the big lower temple on the left, dating from perhaps 3400 BC. It is the best preserved of all the Maltese temples, with several courses of cyclopean masonry above the big dressed boulders at ground level. The plan has two pairs of lobed chambers and a slight niche to end the axis directly in front of the entrance. The two left-hand lobed chambers are linked by a trilith niche of stones decorated by stippling; the inner of these two chambers is subdivided and in it stand two betyls, or pillar altars. Unusual features of the outer right-hand chamber are two portholes or oracle holes cut in the wall, one gives on to a passage leading to the back of the temple, the other to a chamber built inside the mass of the outer walls. This chamber also holds an altar. As in all Maltese temples, the structure is of stone-walled chambers within outer stone walls, with rubble filling between these layers of masonry.

Finally, the middle or upper temple was inserted between the other Mnajdra buildings, perhaps as late as 3200 BC. The basic plan is similar to that of the lower temple beside it, but on a broader scale, with larger spaces and less complexity of detail. One small chamber opens into the massive wall on the left of the inner lobed pair – it contains an altar and again suggests an inner sanctum. Look out for a standing stone to the left of the doorway between the lobed chambers; on it is engraved the outline of a temple, complete with its dome-shaped roof.

Outside the temples, the wide forecourt is dominated by the view of Filfla island. All the large temples had courts like these, and they must surely have been used for great gatherings at important times. It is possible that at least one use of the courts was as a dancing floor; the setting for that archetypal spiral dance which is found the world over. To give just one example, the Bavenda in South Africa have the Deumba or python dance which brings about fertility through cosmic harmony, and is performed by the young virgins of the tribe, '. . . the dancers spiral in the rhythmic movement and sinuous coils of the python. Collapsing and reviving they rest like the forces of nature in the seasonal round of death and rebirth' (Purce 1974). John Fowles, in *Islands*, writes of 'the very ancient spring fertility dance . . . it certainly pre-dated Minoan Crete and was probably originally performed on literal threshing floors, and only later on the symbolic floor of the maze.' He sees it as signifying 'the need to propitiate the forces that control fertility and climatic conditions'. This labyrinthine dance has many layers of meaning. Louis Charpentier speaks of cromlechs as round tables

27. Mnajdra, Malta. View over the temple, which lies down the hill below Hagar Qim, with the sea and Filfla island beyond. The large lower temple of Mnajdra (see plan) was built in about 3400 B.C.

'provided always that it stands over certain surfacings of telluric currents', resembling ritual dance floors, for round dances as a means of identifying with natural rhythms. Writing of the round dance of Chartres Cathedral, which was led by the bishop himself, at Easter, he says, 'In some manner the dancer retraced the cycles of nature to their origin . . . A man who is revolving escapes from space. But to do this is also to go outside time. One may ask oneself to what extent a man who revolves in certain conditions becomes visionary' (Charpentier 1973). And so we come back to the Great Mother, whose work is the magical transformation of souls. She was worshipped in dance, and most of all in orgiastic dance. Neumann again: 'The rite as way begins always as a walked or danced archetype, as image of a spirit, or as a way through the gate of death and birth.'

The archaeologist Colin Renfrew suggests that every pair of temples served as a religious centre for one region of the islands, each region supporting 1000 to 2000 people during the megalithic millennium in Malta (Renfrew 1973, 153 ff). These people grew barley and wheat, and kept sheep, cows and goats. They lived in clay houses, now washed away, and crossed the sea occasionally to trade for obsidian and greenstone axes from Sicily, but for little else. Their tools were of stone or bone only. Another archaeologist, Euan MacKie, has emphasized the local and isolated nature of this Maltese culture, though finding it hard to resist the notion that the sudden eruption of temples – all built between 3500 and 3200 BC – was the result of the arrival of some peaceful but vigorous outsiders. Anatomists have found skeletons which show no trace of the powerful muscles and physical strain usually evident in farmers, and whose teeth seem to have bitten a diet free from grit and coarse fibres (MacKie 1977, 151). This does seem to suggest that there was a priestly caste which used and supervised the temples.

The last major pair of Maltese temples shows the most sophisticated craftsmanship in stone carving of all. Hal Saflieni and Tarxien (pronounced Tarshen) are both entirely hidden among the buildings of one of the suburban towns around Valletta. If the lower temples of the other Malta pairs hint at a connection with the earth, the Hypogeum of Hal Saflieni in the suburb of Pawla is entirely subterranean. The entrance is down a stairway under a building and, from these steps, over twenty rounded chambers open out off each other. After it was discovered in 1902 by workmen cutting cisterns for new houses, its existence was deliberately hidden until the houses were finished, and considerable damage was done. The excavation was completed more

28. The underground Hypogeum of Hal Saflieni, near Valletta, Malta. Architectural detail carved into the solid rock in the so-called Holy of Holies chamber. The temple, in whose side cells 6000 human-beings had been buried, was started in about 3500 BC and enlarged with twenty added spaces over the following five hundred years.

scientifically in 1905–9, when the bones of over 6000 human beings were found in the temple, mostly in the side chambers as if to leave the large rooms free for rituals. Most of these bones were dated at between 3500 and 3000 BC.

The chambers of Hal Saflieni are cut into the solid rock, but walls and ceiling are carved in imitation of the columns, lintel and architraves of the temples above ground. As Gertrude Levy puts it, 'the sacred character of familiar temple construction is artificially imposed to intensify the sanctity of the cave, just as cave sanctity is invoked by the structural forms above ground'. The remains of a painted bull can be seen on one wall. There is a so-called oracle room, with small chambers leading off the main one, and a decoratively detailed doorway from an oval chamber known as the Holy of Holies into a small innermost space, which has walls left rugged and scarcely carved. It seems that this must have been either unfinished or an original holy cave left in its rough state.

The Hypogeum (a word which simply means an underground cham-

29. Tarxien, the hilltop counterpart of the nearby Hypogeum. The central aisle of the south temple, built about 3300 BC, with its famous sculptured decoration. The sculpture is of extraordinary sophistication, yet seems to date from this early period.

ber) has attracted many theories about the function of its chambers and the ceremonies which took place in the areas where no human remains were found. What is known is that the statues of the Great Goddess found here are recumbent, possibly in that sleep of transformation, or like the earth in winter, in the death that goes before rebirth. This may also hint at the symbolism of the in-and-out holes of varying size found in most of the temples, which bore into the darkness of the stone before returning to the surface light.

The above-ground counterpart of Hal Saflieni's depths is Tarxien, a few hundred metres away. Again, the nearby buildings completely obliterate any sense of the original siting, and the four successively built temples sprawl over the site without an overall pattern. The small early temple, a little apart from the others, is as old as Ggantija. The famous large south temple (nearest the site entrance) dates from about 3300 BC

30. Tarxien. The large statue of the Goddess, whose upper parts are lost, with carved panels around her. Tarxien was deserted after 2500 BC and became buried, so the statue must date from before that time.

31. Relief carving of a goat, bull or ram on a panel at Tarxien, done at some time between 3300 and 2500 BC. Other carvings at this temple are unmistakably bulls.

and has a plan like Mnajdra's, with two pairs of lobed chambers and an end niche. The smallest east temple is of much the same date and plan as that just mentioned. Then, as at Mnajdra, a large central temple was inserted between these two, around 3200 BC, but at a different angle of axis. This central temple is entered from one of the inner lobes of the south temple, and it has no less than three pairs of rounded chambers.

It is the carvings and the great statue of the lower part of the fertility goddess herself in the south temple which make Tarxien a matter for wonder. This figure of the goddess (or rather a replica, for the original is in Valletta Museum now) stands just inside the entrance to the temple, her swelling legs running up into a skirt. The statue is broken off below waist level and the upper part has never been found. All around her in the temple are a series of stones carved with the utmost delicacy – spirals abound, but there are other thorn-like motifs too. Most amazing of all are the sophisticated relief carvings of bulls and rows of animals which include pigs, sheep and goats. These are so much unlike anything else found in megalithic monuments anywhere that it is hard to believe that they were not added much later than the Neolithic period. Yet the buried site was only discovered in 1914, and there is no trace of any activity after the temple era ending in 2500 BC, barring a brief use at a different level as a cemetery around the year 2000.

At Tarxien there is one important clue to the Neolithic rituals. A particularly beautiful side altar of the south temple has a removable stone panel in its front. Inside this panel was found a flint knife and the horn of a goat. No sign of human sacrifice exists among the megaliths, but there are other hints of animal sacrifice as well as this one.

Sacrifice, statues of the fertility goddess, and the bull which is her special beast, other symbols of death and rebirth, oracular pronouncements by hidden men or women, large gatherings of people in the courtyards, libations and fires burning before altars – these are the features of Neolithic ritual in Malta which archaeology has suggested as remote indications of their religion. One other point must be mentioned. At the small temple of Tal Qadi a broken fan-shaped stone was found, on whose flat surface are carved radiating lines with crescent moon and groups of stars (Ridley 1971, 67). Recently, the leading Maltese architect Richard England Sant Fournier has been studying the possible use of notches in the hills around the temples as horizon markers for observation of the moon and stars by Neolithic astronomers,

32. Small dolmen on Gozo, Malta, thought to date from around 1800 BC.

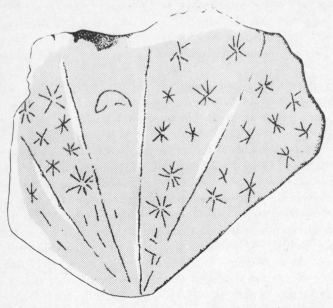

Fig. 17. Representation of a carved stone, 29 by 24 centimetres, apparently depicting stars and crescent moon from an observation point. Found at Tal Qadi, a small temple near the north coast of Malta.

along the lines found in northern Europe (here we must register a protest against the quarrying which is destroying much of Hagar Qim's horizon). Whether or not the possibility of astronomical use is established by research in Malta, the Maltese megalithic culture had ended by about 2500 BC, when the northern astronomers were starting to refine their observatories. Five hundred years later, an early Bronze Age people built a widely scattered group of very small dolmens on the island (in fact Malta can claim both some of the largest and most splendid temples, and some of the puniest and most inept dolmens in all megalithic Europe). After that there appears to be a long gap with little human activity before Phoenician traders settled on the islands and Malta came into the edges of recorded European history.

5 Sardinia

The sunny but often windswept island of Sardinia, now part of Italy, has its own distinct prehistory. Many megalithic structures survive which are unique to the island, while clearly linked to monuments of the period elsewhere. Most of the megaliths are found in the west and north of the island, where the good farming land lies, for much of the east coast and the south-west consists of granite mountains. Sardinia is in an extraordinary position for early navigators; from its southern tip the African coast can be seen on clear days, while its northern end is very near to Corsica, which can in turn be seen from the smaller island of Elba close to the Italian mainland.

Yet Sardinia and Corsica remained uninhabited long after the mainland and Sicily, according to archaeological finds (Guido 1963, 36). The first settlers were apparently the people who developed what is known as the Ozieri culture, which is named after the village in northern Sardinia where the first considerable find of their stone and pottery goods was made in a large natural cave. The culture seems to have grown up from a starting date later than 3000 BC. The earliest megalithic monuments date from around 2500 BC and the culture flourished until about 1700 BC. At some period between 2000 and 1500 BC, many dolmens were built in the northern half of the island and it is not clear whether these were made by the Ozieri people turning away from their customary rock-cut tombs, or by a different people. Finally, in about 1500 BC the nuraghe builders developed their own quite different megalithic architecture which continued until 400 BC and so well into written historical times.

The oldest megalithic monuments in Sardinia are almost all in the north of the island – in or just outside the province of Sássari – and this chapter will concentrate on that area. Apart from the cave burials, the earliest major megalithic remains are the stone circles of Li Muri, right in the north. The place is difficult to find, even with the aid of the good local map in the Touring Club Italiano 1 : 200 000 series.

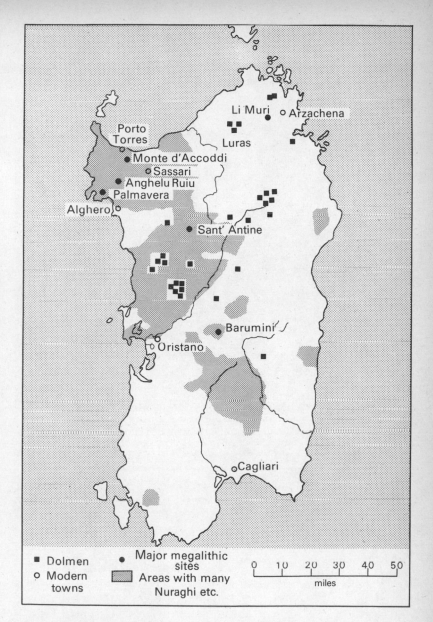

Fig. 18. Outline map of Sardinia, showing the major megalithic sites mentioned, the dolmens recorded on the island and the areas where the Nuraghe or Tower people built most (Derived from Guido).

105

33. Sardinia. The four intersecting and paved stone circles of Li Muri, west of Arzachena, in the north-east of the island. Each circle has an oblong cell of stone slabs at its centre. Human remains were found in only one of these, and the platforms suggest use for other rites of various kinds. The circles are thought to date from around 2500 B.C.

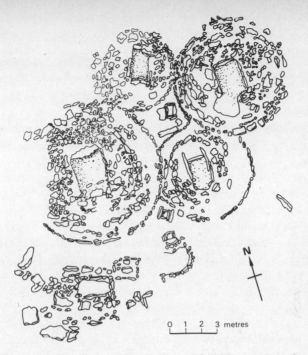

Fig. 19. Plan of the intersecting paved stone circles at Li Muri, Arzachena, Sardinia.

From the small town of Arzachena, near the east coast, take the minor road towards Luogosanto for eight kilometres. Before reaching St Oddastru railway station, a yellow tourist signpost points along a car track to the right to 'Necropolo Li Muri'. This track winds through boulder-strewn hills until it forks beyond a roadside farmhouse (the right-hand fork leads to a fine Giant's Tomb, which will be mentioned later). The left-hand road rises past one farmhouse and straight through the yard of another. The track then takes to the steep hills, passing through two farm gates and deteriorating in quality. Over the top of a steep hill and perhaps a hundred metres beyond, the circles can be glimpsed over a wall on the right. They are not signposted here.

The five intersecting circles of Li Muri are not large – the largest is only 25 feet (7.6 metres) in diameter – but they are impressive in themselves and in their siting. They lie in a position typical of megalithic monuments in many parts of Europe – on a platform on the downward slope of a spur, with the horizon surrounded by hills except on one more open side – although the site is unusually high. In the centre of each circle is a cist (a simple small chamber of stone slabs) with stone paving around it and a surrounding circle of upright slabs mixed with slender standing stones. When excavated, human bones were found in only one of the chambers, but the other finds in the cists included flint knives, axes and beads of various stones, pottery and a great deal of red ochre stain.

The position of the circles seems strongly linked to the sky, for ritual invocation and perhaps for celestial observations aligning the small standing stones with markers on the rugged horizon. The stones within each circle definitely appear to be the remains of paving, rather than of a cairn (as has been suggested), and this may imply that the site was an important place for seasonal ceremonies and perhaps for ritual dancing such as was described in the chapter on Malta. The fact that the circles intersect should not be dismissed as chance or carelessness, for patterns such as these occur on a small scale in rock-carvings on megaliths in several parts of Europe. It is thought (Guido 1963, 40) that Li Muri dates from early in the Ozieri period, perhaps from about 2500 BC.

The nearest megalithic sites remotely comparable with Li Muri are in Corsica, southern France and eastern Spain, and this raises the question of who the Ozieri people were. There is good evidence that the Beaker people from northern Europe contributed much to their later culture, but there are also strong links with the eastern Mediterranean. Many figurines of this period, possibly used as idols, have been found in Sardinia; some are similar to Cycladic statuettes – flat-fronted with only the nose and breasts in relief – while others are rounded in forms more typical of mainland France and other parts of north-western Europe. The skulls found here show quite different shapes in various settlements of the same date. It is likely that the unique forms of many Sardinian megaliths were the result of a stimulating mixture of settlers arriving from the north and from the eastern Mediterranean.

The Ozieri people buried most of their dead in rock-cut chambers. The most celebrated of the rock-cut cemeteries is Anghelu Ruiu, which is nine kilometres north of Alghero (a port on the west coast) on the left-hand side of the road to Porto Tórres. This is by no means a dramatic site. A slight cliff along one side of a meadow, near a river in low countryside, contains some of the rock-cut tombs. But most of the thirty-five chambers are cut in the sides of trenches slit through the flat grass and earth of the meadow and into the rock beneath. The tomb chambers are not large; most can be entered easily enough on

34. The bulls' head frieze over one of the tombs in the Anghelu Ruiu cemetery, near Alghero, Sardinia. Calibrated dates ranging from 2200 to 1700 BC have been yielded by material in the thirty-five small rock-cut tombs, three of which have carvings of bulls' heads.

hands and knees through doorways, some of which are carved to imitate smoothly dressed trilithons. What makes Anghelu Ruiu famous are the carvings of long-horned bulls' heads in and around three of the tombs (those numbered XIX, XX bis and XXX) and the rich grave goods found inside. These goods date from 2200 to 1700 BC and included many flint tools, mace-heads, arrowheads, axes and beads. But there were also such unexpected metal objects as silver rings, copper daggers thought to be imported from Spain, an awl probably from southern France, a copper ring of an eastern European type and an axe from the British Isles. Whether the carved bulls' heads here, as in Malta, are linked with the Great Goddess, or are symbols of a later Sun cult, as several writers have suggested, is open to debate.

What does seem clear is that we have here again a mixture of eastern and northern influences and products, and this is confirmed in a much more mysterious way at the last great sanctuary of the Ozieri culture.

This monument is the man-made mound called Monte d'Accoddi,

35. Monte d'Accoddi, near Porto Torres, Sardinia. The 40 feet (13 metres) high mound was built of cyclopean drystone walls about 1700 BC. Under the grass and eroded earth, it takes a form like a two-tier square ziggurat, with a ramp (on the left of this picture) running from ground level in the south up to the top of the monument.

along an inadequately signposted track off the right-hand side of the motorway seven kilometres south-east of Porto Tórres, on the way to Sássari. This area is near the middle of a rolling plain with distant mountains around three sides and the sea on the fourth. It is only when one reaches the Monte itself that one realizes that, like numerous other sites, it is on a low spur which drops into a valley below the level of the plain.

Monte d'Accoddi is about 40 feet (12 metres) high today, with two stages of cyclopean drystone walling (the upper stage in bad repair and very overgrown now) forming a structure like a ziggurat of two steps, square in plan. It is oriented four-square to the cardinal points of the compass, possibly calculated from the equinoctial sunrise. The site probably dates from about 1700 BC. From the southward side of the mound, a long straight ramp with stone walls rises gradually above the lower step and continues to the upper stage, where one emerges on to the summit, facing northwards. As one reaches the top, the far mountains are at one's back and sides. In front is the sea, while the great bowl of sky overhead dominates everything. Archaeologists have found no trace of a chamber or an entrance to the mound and recognize that in their absence the Monte must be regarded as an observatory or as an 'altar or high place' (Guido 1963, 59). Certainly, it has the type of sacred atmosphere felt at very particular places on the earth's surface.

The surroundings of the Monte d'Accoddi have been partly excavated and the signs of a considerable sacred centre can be seen. A dolmen lies close to the south-eastern corner and a carefully smoothed menhir lies on the other side of the approach ramp, formerly one of several standing stones in the vicinity. There are the partly excavated foundations of many small structures, perhaps residential, and several mysterious carved stones. The most impressive of these is a great boulder carved into the shape of an egg and then cut through on a curving three-dimensional line of great geometrical subtlety. Much of the site remains unexcavated but where the spur drops away to the valley, a ramp continues the level of the Monte's base for about 100 metres into mid-air in a south-south-westerly direction. One leaves Monte d'Accoddi awed by the experience of space and liberation upon reaching the top of the mound and tantalized by the hints of more strange remains in the unexcavated parts of the surroundings.

Both the design of the sacred mound and the small idols found on the site show obvious links between the Monte and the eastern Mediterranean. But again, other finds indicate contact with the Beaker

36. Monte d'Accoddi, Sardinia. The large egg-shaped boulder, with a curving cut right through it, is one of many mysterious features of the partly excavated area around the mound. A dolmen sits close to the mound and there are several earthwork ramps nearby.

people from the north. The dolmen (these are generally called *stazzone* in Sardinia) beside the Monte d'Accoddi leads on to the next stage of Sardinian prehistory, for this type of structure seems to have replaced the rock-cut chambers of the Anghelu Ruiu type at some point after 2000 BC. As can be seen from the map, they are found throughout the centre of the north half of the island. Margaret Guido and D. Mackenzie have put forward the theory that the well-known

Giants' Tombs of Sardinia evolved from the dolmen in its mound, which had itself been brought by settlers from mainland Europe via Corsica or from Malta.

Whether that is so or not, mention of the Giants' Tombs takes us on to the Tower People, otherwise known as the Nuraghe builders or the Shardana. The implication of Mrs Guido's argument is that we do not have to accept previous assumptions that these were new people who arrived and settled in Sardinia about 1500 BC. The formidable Nuragic culture more probably developed at about that time among the native Sardinian megalith builders, perhaps partly influenced by dolmen-building settlers who were soon integrated into the island population.

These Nuragic people of the Bronze Age will generally be called the Tower People in this book and some explanation about them is needed here, since this is the first section on an important group of late megalith builders. Unlike their peaceful predecessors, the tower builders appear to have become a race of warriors. Early on, they invaded Corsica (where they are depicted in statue menhirs and are nowadays called the Torreans) and the Balearic Islands (where they are usually referred to as the Talayot culture), and we shall meet them again in those chapters. On each island they developed quite different megalithic monuments for sacred purposes, but in all cases they built chambered round towers of cyclopean stone structure for defence and for living quarters. In Sardinia, these towers are called *nuraghe* in the singular, *nuraghi* in the plural, and their builders' civilization is termed the Nuragic culture. It is worth mentioning that the building techniques used for the sanctuary walls at Monte d'Accoddi were already advanced enough for the construction of nuraghi.

The map shows the areas where most nuraghi survive in Sardinia. The high stone structures started as single towers – many remain like this – and were expanded into multiple towers, often with complexes of circular huts and strong walls around them, if their resident population grew. In the north of the island, one of the best multiple examples is Palmavera, beside the road eleven kilometres west along the coast from Alghero. The tower is a double one, with fine chambers inside. It has subsidiary stone structures between the towers and in the walled living enclosure around them. The nuraghi of Sardinia are too numerous to list here, but one of the most impressive is Sant'Antine, close to the motorway southwards from Sássari towards Cagliari, near Torralba railway station. This has one massive high tower and a lower broad triangular tower built outwards around it. The most complex of all the

37. A typical nuraghe of the sort built of cyclopean drystone masonry in many parts of Sardinia between 1500 and about 600 BC. This single tower is east of Castelsardo.

38. The double nuraghe of Palmavera, near Alghero in Sardinia, and its surrounding complex of smaller buildings and circular stone houses. The multiple towers were developed gradually over the centuries around 1000 BC.

nuraghi is Su Nuraxi at Barumini, still farther south. Barumini has been fully excavated, revealing a central tower, a tremendous square lower structure around it with protruding towers at each corner, and the remains of a seemingly endless complex of walls and circular or irregular stone huts beyond.

The so-called Giants' Tombs appear to have been not only the collective burial-places but the chief religious centres of the Tower People in Sardinia. They consist of a forecourt with a curved frontage of high megalithic upright slabs or cyclopean wall against a man-made mound containing a stone chamber. The central stone of the frontage is usually the highest, with a small entrance cut through it at ground level; it is normally round-topped and has two blank recesses carved into its upper face. The forecourt was clearly used for religious ceremonies, not necessarily limited to the times of human burials. Some of the Giants' Tombs have frontages of cyclopean masonry, rather than standing stones. Again, there are too many Giants' Tombs in Sardinia to describe more than the type here.

Sometimes the mound over a Giant's Tomb has been eroded away,

39. Typical megalithic forecourt frontage of a Giant's Tomb, in this case with its earth mound vanished, near the Li Muri circles. These Giants' Tombs were built all over Sardinia by the nuraghe tower builders between 1500 and about 600 BC.

as at the tomb near the Li Muri circles, so that the chamber within is exposed. In these cases, the basis for the theory that they developed from dolmens can be seen. Some of the dolmens on the island are long in form and, if they were all originally covered by mounds, it is clear the Tower People could have simply added the megalithic frontage and the forecourt to the older idea from mainland Europe.

Apart from the nuraghi themselves and the Giants' Tombs, the Tower People built a number of other types of structure. Towards the end of the period, it appears that they even built temples showing Greek influence – two examples have been found at Serra Orrios near Dorgali and one at Cuccureddi near Esterzili. More typical and more interesting are the fifty sophisticated sanctuaries dating from 1000 BC onwards, with domes of stone built over sacred springs and wells, scattered over all the island. Some of these waters are still credited with

40. The chamber inside the Giant's Tomb near Li Muri, now exposed by the erosion of its mound.

healing powers and bronze figures of humans, animals and weapons have been found around them. Good examples can be found at Golfo degli Aranci near Olbia and at Sant'Anastasia near Sardara. Other forms of sanctuary can also be seen, mysterious in their purposes, but showing evidence of animal sacrifice and rites associated with a bronze double axe. The double axe was originally an emblem of the Great Goddess. Some say that it represented the settled farming ways, perhaps from its use in clearing the forests. But in Sardinia at this late period its significance may well have changed a good deal.

Because they survived well into Classical Greek times, more is known of the tower builders than of any other megalithic people, although there is little information about their religion. As the Shardana, they were widely known as mercenary soldiers throughout the Mediterranean. Bronze statues survive showing their armed warriors with fantastic helmets. The name Shardan can be linked with Sardinia as early as 700 BC. In the fourth century BC Aristotle, and later Ptolemy, tell of tombs in Sardinia dedicated to their heroes. Strabo mentions their raids on the Etruscans of mainland Italy. Diodorus Siculus, the Greek historian of about 50 BC tells of the Phoenician settlements in Sardinia after 800 BC. He goes on to relate its eventual military occupation by Carthage, which led to the sacking of the major nuraghi in about 500 BC and the end of the Nuragic culture during the following century.

6 Corsica – Filitosa

The wildly mountainous island of Corsica, a far more savage land than its close neighbour, Sardinia, was thinly settled by Neolithic farmers from soon after 4000 BC until their conquest by the invading Tower People at some time around 1400 BC. There are two main megalithic sites on the island, as well as many scattered menhirs and encircled cists. Of these two sites, one was left alone by the Tower People, while the other – the famous sanctuary of Filitosa – was taken over and reconstructed by these late megalith builders, who probably came from Sardinia.

For over a thousand years the early Corsican farmers in the southern half of the island apparently built only low circles of standing stone slabs with a cist, or stone chamber, in the centre and usually with a single menhir nearby. These are broadly similar to the multiple rings of Li Muri in Sardinia, but one example south-west of Porto Vecchio, at Tivolaggiu, has two concentric circles. No human bones have been found in these cists – they may have been consumed by the acid soil, or the various articles found may not be grave goods but served some other ritual purpose.

During the years between 2300 and 1500 BC, a unique type of megalithic monument developed in Corsica. This was the statue-menhir; a standing stone with its top carved to represent the human face and other features.

The earliest statue-menhirs are primitive in their carving, but the craftsmanship became steadily more sophisticated. The latest highly stylized examples may date from after 1500 BC, since these are always taken to represent warriors of the Tower People – who had occupied much of Corsica by then and were shortly to put an end to the earlier megalithic culture.

The major group of surviving early megaliths in Corsica is near the west coast, south of the seaside town of Propriano (which makes a good

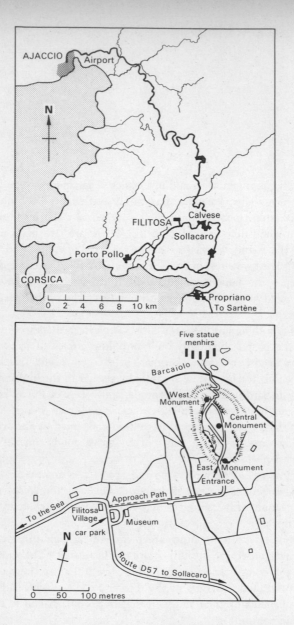

Fig. 20. Outline map of part of Corsica and plan of the Filitosa megalithic site.

centre for visiting these sites and Filitosa). A main road zigzags up for twelve kilometres to the inland village of Sartène. From there the very narrow D48 road twists southwards through the mountains for another eighteen kilometres to Cauria – a place that scarcely exists, but near which are the megaliths, including the great dolmen of Fontanaccia with the stump of a nearby menhir. This suggests that the dolmen form may have grown directly, in about 2000 BC, from the local encircled cist and menhir tradition, perhaps stimulated by overseas ideas recounted by traders. Indeed, another dolmen in Settiva has a circle of standing stones around it. But the particular interest of Fontanaccia is that there are alignments of uncarved standing stones near it. The stones in these alignments are graded from about man-height down to quite small stones. Of course this suggests a link with the great Carnac alignments in Brittany, and the possibility of an astronomical function. The date of about 2000 BC fits well enough, but we are immediately faced with the problem that these lines (and those of the several other alignments in Corsica) point due north–south, rather than on a bearing around south-west to north-east as in Brittany.

The whole question of direction is puzzling in the Corsican megaliths. Fontanaccia and all other dolmens have entrances which face south-east or east-south-east, except for the dolmens which are actually part of an alignment of standing stones – the entrances face due south in these cases, along the line of stones. In some places, notably at Palaggiu a few kilometres north-west of Cauria, statue-menhirs are found in an alignment; where this occurs, the statue-menhir always faces east. Near the alignment at Palaggiu there is one of the late examples of a stone circle around a cist (cupmarked in this case) and these monuments probably continued to be built at the same time as the dolmens and alignments (Grinsell 1975, 187).

It is clear that in Corsica the megaliths of around 2000 BC take local forms which are linked remotely to those of mainland Europe. As at Li Muri in Sardinia, the circles speak of a cult looking up into the skies. Alignments also hint at a celestial function, but those in Corsica have not yet been studied for any astronomical significance. Later in this book we shall see that in Germany there are great stone rows oriented due east–west, and the north–south direction of the Corsican lines suggests another significance for such cardinal orientation before knowledge of the compass (but not necessarily before an ability to find the north). The statue-menhirs demand another speculative approach. It is not known whether they are monuments to individuals or objects of worship. Their usual east-facing direction may concern sunrise or their makers' origins. One theory is that these people believed that a human likeness would bring that individual's powers to the community as a whole, for they made statue-menhirs of the Tower People when they were threatened by those fierce warriors. If this is so, it does seem odd that the Tower People knocked down many of the statue-menhirs and used them as building-stones. Perhaps they removed the less flattering images of themselves.

It is the work of these Tower People (generally called the Torréens in France) that can chiefly be seen today at the most famous and beautiful megalithic site in Corsica. Filitosa is a few kilometres west of the mountainous main road from Propriano northwards to Ajaccio, the capital city of Corsica. A minor road winds steeply down through the villages of Sollacaro and Calvese to the well-marked site with its small museum and surrounding hamlet. A footpath between the fields leads to the tree-covered enclosure, which is above a stream on a spur projecting into a great bowl in the mountains. The Taravo river is close by.

When visiting Filitosa, it helps to keep in mind from the beginning that this sacred site was occupied by megalithic people from perhaps 4000 until about 1400 BC, after which the Tower People completely rebuilt it during their occupation which lasted until after 800 BC, and perhaps as late as 500 BC. So none of the many erect statue-menhirs on the site are in their original positions; they were found buried during excavations following Filitosa's discovery in 1954 and re-erected where the excavators saw fit.

Except at the entrance end, the long, almost level, top of the spur has steep sides falling away in all directions. This made it easily defensible, which may have been no particular advantage during the generally peaceful Neolithic period, but was clearly valuable during the more turbulent Bronze Age. Perhaps for this reason, the Tower People built a structure around the entrance which is now called the *Monument Est* and was probably fortified. The gateway is narrow and inside the site, we wander under the olive trees through the remains of enclosures built partly into the ground, the bedrock rearing up, sometimes hollowed into shallow caves. On the left, the southern side, a number of dwellings of the Tower People have been excavated.

Halfway along the length of the rough platform on top of the spur, there is the so-called *Monument Central*. This is the remains of a cyclopean tower of 1300 BC which originally consisted of a circular platform perhaps about 7 feet (2 metres) high, with a chambered round

41. Corsica. The rocky spur which is the site of Filitosa, the megalithic sanctuary inhabited in three stages from about 4000 BC until 500 BC.

42. Filitosa. The cyclopean circular monument built by the Tower People or Torreans after 1400 BC. The statue menhirs, erected there before 1500 BC by the earlier megalith builders, were found buried in the foundations of this tower when it was excavated – they were re-erected at random. The menhirs may have stood in lines on the site before this Central Monument was built.

tower rising from its centre. The Tower People built chambered towers (like their nuraghi in Sardinia) wherever they settled in Corsica. But this central monument at Filitosa was probably a religious building – rather than for habitation or defence – and archaeologists believe that it was roofed by a cyclopean vault similar to the same people's structures over sacred springs in Sardinia (Grosjean 1975, 11).

The most striking thing about the central monument today is the large number of standing stones and statue-menhirs of 2000 to 1500 BC which have been set upright around it. These were discovered in the walls of the central monument when it was excavated – buried there by

43. Detail of one of the statue menhirs on the Central Monument of Filitosa.

the Tower People when they rebuilt the site at some time before 1000 BC. The crudity of some of these statue-menhirs can be compared with the fine late work shown in others, such as the famous one which now stands beside the path from the road to the site itself.

It is not known how these many menhirs were arranged before the Torreans threw them down, but there seem two possibilities. Either the round central monument stands on the previous site of a stone circle with a cist at its centre – a type of monument which has been mentioned at other places in Corsica, Sardinia and southern France – or else the

44. The great rock outcrop, which seems carved rather than eroded, forming the core of the Western Monument of Filitosa. The cyclopean structures around the rock – which itself was probably revered – date from the period between 1400 and 900 BC. These structures form entrances to chambers, which may be much older, under the great rock.

45. The half-ring of statue menhirs from the Filitosa site, recently erected here on the flatter ground of the valley below the site itself where they were found.

menhirs were arranged in alignments. If the last explanation is correct, the lines presumably ran across the length of the spur, in the north–south direction of other Corsican alignments.

The most impressive of the three main monuments at Filitosa is the *Monument Ouest* at the tip of the site. This consists of a great natural outcrop of rock well over 20 feet (6 metres) high, with a complex of cyclopean chambers forming a roundish platform on one side of it. That great rock appears to be the centre of the Filitosa cult, for it is carved with vertical channels which seem man-made, has a large rounded niche above-ground on one side and small underground chambers beneath it on the other. Its importance must pre-date the Tower People and one is reminded of similar cult outcrops in northern Europe – notably one in Belgium – and the combination of rearing rock with underground cells has echoes of the sky and earth pairings of the Maltese temples.

Beyond the west monument, the tip of the spur falls away sharply and one can see again that typical positioning of sacred megalithic sites in the landscape. The siting on a spur is classic and the horizon is formed by hills – in this case real mountains – on three sides, with the fourth side more open. The river, with quick access to the sea, is within easy reach. This was apparently an important consideration for practical or symbolic reasons at megalithic sites.

On the slopes of the Filitosa spur and on other outcrops across the small valley are a number of boulders which were adapted as rock shelters by the Tower People. In the valley below the west monument, five slender statue-menhirs have been arranged attractively around a clump of trees since the excavations were carried out. In some cases, statue-menhirs seem phallic, but on close examination there are almost always worn facial features to be seen.

Filitosa is among the most lovely settings of all megalithic sites, evidently a sacred place for both the early and the late megalith-building peoples who used it. It must be said, however, that the special feeling of holiness which pervades megalithic monuments such as Hagar Qim and Monte d'Accoddi in the Mediterranean and most such places in northern Europe, is not felt at Filitosa. Perhaps sheer numbers of visitors make it difficult to contact such an elusive atmosphere, as so often happens at Stonehenge – even in the best conditions it is frequently hard to distinguish objective from subjective sensations in these places. But it also seems possible that the harmony with place achieved by the Neolithic megalith builders of around 2000 BC was disrupted by the cult structures of the Bronze Age people who superseded them. However, the following chapter will show that, at least in Menorca, the Tower People were quite capable of making religious places of intensely sacred feeling.

7   The Balearic Islands – Menorca and Majorca

The group of islands east of Valencia, known as the Baliares even before Rome conquered them in 123 BC, have some of the finest late megaliths in all Europe. Of the four major islands, Ibiza and Formentera do not appear to have been much inhabited before the Carthaginian colonests came in 654 BC, but Majorca contains notable remains and Menorca has the most evocative megalithic monuments on Spanish soil. These islands are among the most popular of Mediterranean holiday resorts, yet their early monuments are little known except among Spaniards.

The earliest settlements of the Balearics have been radiocarbon dated at 4900 BC (calibrated). These seem to have been poor people, who lived in caves and rock shelters. The first burials known to archaeologists are in natural caves, which abound on the islands, and occasionally in man-made caves of one chamber. These tombs – Vernissa, near Santa Margarita in Majorca shows good examples – are of the late Neolithic period and range from 2300 to 1800 BC (Pericot 1972, 40). A very small number of dolmens also exist, one in Majorca and four in Menorca (the best is Sa Comerma de Sa Garita at Torre d'En Goumes, in Alayor province). These have no capstones surviving and may represent a shortlived attempt at colonization from the mainland at some time before 1500 BC.

During the Copper and early Bronze Ages in 1800 to 1500 BC, the inhabitants built many rock-cut chambers in Menorca and especially in Majorca. These are shaped like upturned boats within the rock. Their solid vaults are well smoothed and their plans, many with side-chambers, are strikingly like those of the much earlier Grotte des Fées group near Arles in southern France (see Chapter 2). The eminent archaeologist Pericot has described opening one of these chambers and finding bones in it (Pericot 1972, 32) but the great majority had no signs of human remains and some were undoubtedly used for habitation. Good

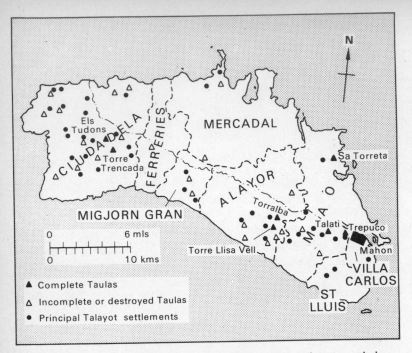

Fig. 21. Outline map of Menorca, with the main Talayot tower settlements marked as circles and the Taulas marked as T for complete monuments or – for incomplete or destroyed examples. The dotted line indicates the boundary between the good farming land in the south and the poor rocky land in the north. Derived from Pericot.

examples can be seen at Cala San Vicente in Majorca (Grinsell 1975, 190).

Sometimes a later boat-shaped 'navetiform' chamber of cyclopean masonry structure can be found above ground near these rock-cut shelters and this suggests that the Talayotic culture, which followed the Neolithic period, took the shape of its burial-places from the man-made caves.

The Talayotic culture started with invasions of around 1500 BC and continued throughout the Bronze and Iron Ages until about 500 BC. After that, the culture lingered on in a reduced form until the Romans arrived. The monuments of the Talayotic period are very different from those of earlier times and there has been a good deal of discussion about the identity of the invaders. The most common of their structures is the round cyclopean tower called a 'talayot' or 'talaia' in the

46. Menorca. The cyclopean tower or talayot of Trepuco, just outside Mahon. This is one of many such talayots (which were defensive and residential) built by the Tower people (who were probably from Sardinia) in the Balearic islands between 1500 and some time after 1000 BC.

Balearics. These are very like Sardinian nuraghi, while the 'naveta' tombs mentioned above are in some ways very similar to some of the cyclopean Giants' Tombs of Sardinia, adapted to local conditions. Within historical times there was a tribe called the Balari in Sardinia. It is now generally agreed that these invaders were the Tower People or Shardanas, who emerged in Sardinia a little before 1500 BC and conquered Corsica at much the same time as the Talayotic culture appeared in the Balearic islands. This culture reached its peak between 900 and 600 BC.

The word 'talayot' means a watchtower, but in fact almost all of the hundreds of towers in Majorca and Menorca have chambers within them and were probably inhabited. Most are circular, but a few are square in plan. They were certainly used as fortifications and the settlements around them have strong walls. In Majorca, the talayotic site called Ses Paisses, a kilometre south-east of Arta, includes a central talayot tower, outer walls and four megalithic gateways around the dwellings in the enclosure. Els Antigors, near Ses Salinas, has several towers and extensive walls – many bronze axes, daggers and tools were discovered here.

The known religious sites in Majorca are not so highly developed as those in Menorca, but at Almallatux near Escorca there are sanctuaries consisting of walled courts with pillars in the centre – each pillar is formed by a long standing stone with a smaller and slightly wider horizontal stone on top. These rather resemble the Menorcan 'taulas' which will be described later, but there are no true taulas or navetas in Majorca - these are unique to Menorca.

Menorca is not a large island – it is no more than sixty kilometres from the capital Mahòn at one end to Ciudadela at the other. The map shows an irregular line running the length of the island, which divides the infertile hilly northern area of ancient Devonian rock from the prosperous farms in the more densely populated southern plain, where the soil is good and the rock a Miocene limestone. The typical trees are ilex, wild olives and pines – cactus is widespread today, but was brought here only after the discovery of America. Menorca is subject to violent winds from the north, and probably has been so ever since a change in the weather of southern Europe in about 1000 BC.

The map also shows that most of the major talayotic settlements were in the fertile southern half of Menorca, so despite their warlike characteristics the Tower People here were clearly farmers first and mercenaries or pirates second. The fortified settlements show a need for defence so perhaps they and their neighbours in Majorca were on hostile and predatory terms. They were certainly able sailors and accomplished builders. Metal was scarce for them, for there are few copper deposits on the islands.

The Menorcan talayotic people continued the custom of their predecessors in burying most of their dead in rock-cut chambers. But other burials were in fine cyclopean stone structures known as navetas (it has already been suggested that the shape of these monuments was inherited from that of the older rock-cut chambers).

There are many navetas on the island, but the finest is that of Els Tudons (the wood pigeons). It lies a short distance along a signposted track to the left off the road from Mahòn, four kilometres before it reaches Ciudadela. It is positioned on a shallow spur in very slightly rolling country, with its entrance façade – which is a little concave – facing west-south-west. The cyclopean stonework is quite smoothly dressed, much more so than that of the talayots, and the flat-sterned boat shape (the name 'naveta' was invented by the antiquary Ramis in 1818) is immediately evident, whether it is intentional or not. Inside the small entrance, the structure is more complicated than can be seen from without. A little ante-chamber gives access to the main room and, above head height, to a shallow upper chamber which seems more like an insulating gap between the two drystone vaults. The main space

47. The entrance front at the flattened end of the naveta of Els Tudons, near Ciudadela, Menorca. The navetas were the collective burial monuments of the Tower people, and were built during the same years as the talayots. The name naveta was given to these structures because they are shaped like upturned boats, flattened at one end and pointed at the other.

below has a shelf or altar ledge at the far end. When this architectural *tour de force* was excavated in 1958, the remains of more than 100 human-beings, with simple bronze and bone grave goods, were found beneath the chamber.

The complex designs of the navetas were perhaps built only for funerary rites, for these were not the principal sanctuaries of the Tower People in Menorca. The temples of their talayot settlements were circular enclosures, with a ring of standing stones around the

133

48. Interior of the naveta of Els Tudons. The photograph shows the pointed end of the long lower chamber – a low upper chamber runs above it.

great T-shaped megaliths called taulas. There were twenty-eight of these in the island, two of which will be described here, while the remainder are marked on the map.

The largest taula (the name means 'table' in Catalan, for obvious reasons), and the most easily accessible, is beside the talayot of Trepuco. This is on the outskirts of Mahòn itself. Tower and taula can be seen on the left of the main road to San Luis, just beyond the built-up area, and the site is reached along narrow and insufficiently signposted side roads. It stands on a slight rise, the lower part of the round tower well preserved and the taula enclosure a few metres beyond it. Within its circle of tall irregular standing stones, the taula rises 13 feet (4 metres), with its capstone higher still.

As with all taulas, it is very broad in one dimension, very narrow in the other. Both orthostat and capstone are slightly trapezoidal in outline, and one face of the Trepuco taula is decorated with roughly

49. The taula of Trepuco, outside Mahon, Menorca. The taulas, with their great capstoned megaliths and surrounding ring of standing stones, were the ritual sanctuaries of the Tower people and were built during the same centuries as the talayots. The human figure on the encircling wall gives an idea of the scale.

50. Detail of the narrow end of the taula at Trepuco.

parallel diagonal lines, fairly evenly spaced. These lines have an odd quality, somehow suggesting natural lines of cleavage rather than the normal linear decorations on megaliths, which are usually quite broad shallow lines. Trepuco is an impressive monument, with a complex of outbuildings around the taula sanctuary, but the site is ill tended and too worn for much sacred atmosphere to survive.

The other great taula to be covered here is a far more atmospheric place, partly perhaps because it is remarkably difficult to find. The talayot of Talatí de Dalt lies on a hill a few hundred metres off the main road from Mahòn to Alayor, along a turning to the left less than three kilometres beyond the edge of Mahòn. The site is not indicated on the main road although there is a signpost to a restaurant. The minor road reaches a fork, at which one turns right and soon finds

51. Talati de Dalt, near Mahon, Menorca. The approach to the taula sanctuary, with the pierced menhir on the left.

some steps over a wall on the left – again unsigned, but the tree-covered hill can be seen above the road.

Talatí is a very complex site, comprising five talayot towers, some stone circles, circular houses with covered courts supported by large stone pillars and ten underground chambers scattered among the trees, apart from the taula enclosure. From the rough entrance steps, a path leads through a gate and past the remains of what appears to be a megalithic gateway. The ground then slopes upwards to the right, providing a wide and gradual approach avenue between the trees. Rounding a corner, a single menhir, pierced by a hole, appears ahead. Beside it there is a stretch of cyclopean masonry in the long modern wall along the edge of the abrupt drop which surrounds most of the ancient settlement. The grass avenue between the trees and the wall widens – first the big main talayot and then the taula gradually appear among the foliage.

This main talayot stands on the very peak of the hill. From its top there is a good view of the taula sanctuary below and of the surround-

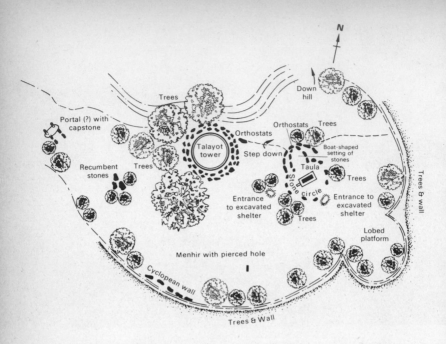

Fig. 22. Talati de Dalt, Menorca. Sketch plan of part of the large site, showing the Taula sanctuary and the main Talayot.

ing countryside. The tower slopes inwards sharply as it rises – it is in fact chambered, although that cannot be seen today. But it is the taula and its surroundings which draw the attention.

Although it is not as tall as the Trepuco monument, the Talatí taula has a thunderous presence, partly derived from its more massive proportions, which make it appear far the most powerful of all these great Menorcan megaliths. It is also one of a small number of taulas with an extra stone pillar supporting the capstone, but not for functional reasons – in the case of Talatí, this pillar is set diagonally against one end of the capstone, with a smaller stone cushioning it. The standing stones forming the circle around the taula are exceptionally large, too; great menhirs of rough-textured rock half hidden by the trees around the sanctuary. Beyond the taula, a strange setting of low stones, like the bows of a boat can be seen within the enclosure. Outside it, there are small entrances to a number of underground chambers. Talatí, like the

52. The main cyclopean tower or talayot of Talati de Dalt.

other taulas and the navetas, probably dates from 1000 BC or a century or two later.

Talatí is among a select few of the finest and most mysterious of all megalithic sites in southern Europe, only a handful of Maltese and Sardinian places ranking with it. Huge and ancient olive trees grow around the site, some of them partly embedded in the relatively modern wall. We felt an unchanging presence here, cherishing and informing the vast stones, the trees, the whole mound. Mysterious it is, because although the Balearic peoples are mentioned fairly often in Greek and Latin literature, nothing is recorded of their religion. Diodorus and others mention their famous sling-throwers as mercenaries from 400 BC

53. The broad face of the great taula of Talati, with its massive circle of standing stones and the strange diagonal stone against one end of the capstone. Probably built around 1000 BC.

54. The sanctuary of Talati de Dalt, showing the narrow end of the taula.

onwards, and Hannibal enlisted about 2000 of them during his roundabout expedition to attack Rome in the third century BC. But there is
no mention of their beliefs or ceremonies. Margaret Murray excavated
Trepuco earlier in this century and found only ashes of uncertain age.
Many bronze bulls have been found at various sites, hinting at a bull
cult – as has been suggested for Malta and Sardinia. It has been pro-
posed that the taulas are representations of bulls' heads, stylized beyond
recognition. This seems possible – since the bull is so widespread in
myths all around the Mediterranean, first linked to the Great Goddess
and later to the superseding Sun – especially if placed within a circular
enclosure or ring of standing stones as the taulas are. As at the paved
platforms of Li Muri in Sardinia, ritual 'dancing floors' may be suggested by the form of the sanctuaries. There is no sign yet recorded that
the Tower People were involved in methodical observation of celestial
bodies, although great pillars of stone carved from bedrock, or formed
by superimposed boulders, are found on many Menorcan cliffs – these
could be astronomical or navigational markers. The circles of tall standing stones around the taulas doubtless had great symbolic and ritual

importance, as is the case with those in the British Isles, whatever their other functions.

Finally, some other works produced by the Tower People should be mentioned. The roofed enclosures, courts with roofs supported by pillars of stones (which get wider towards the top), have been noted at Talatí de Dalt, but are a widespread type of structure unique to Menorca. There are also simpler enclosures in remote places, possibly sanctuaries but more likely refuges for times of great crisis. And cut into a number of rock faces, in groups of up to fifty in one place, there are hundreds of oval cavities little more than the size of a human head – these are known as 'capades de Moro' locally, after a legend which says that they were the work of Moors who crashed their heads against the rock to form them.

It is clear from the chapters on Sardinia, Corsica and the Balearics that the same people were probably responsible for the late megalithic cultures that lasted for about a thousand years in those islands. Their towers are similar wherever they built them, though only in Sardinia did they achieve the multiple forms of which Barumini is the extreme example. Their other monuments are so varied that the conclusion must be that they took the local building customs wherever they went and developed these into unique megalithic types of their own. Of these, the taulas of Menorca hold the highest place and make fitting ending to this survey of megaliths in southern Europe.

Northern Europe

General

It is evident that the thousands of years of megalithic building in southern Europe were divided into many stages and many local or regional cultures which had some degree of contact with each other. The same is true of northern Europe, although some of the cultures in the north covered very extensive areas.

The first Neolithic farming communities emerged in north-western Europe (apart from France and Britain) via the long river basin of the Danube. A village of this period at Geelen in Holland, whose radiocarbon date must now be calibrated to give a date of a century or two after 5000 BC (De Laet 1962, 59), had five Long Houses with rows of thick posts supporting their roofs and walls of daubed wattle or squared tree trunks. This Danubian culture appears from the datable evidence to have spread from Bohemia across central Germany to the North Sea. It cultivated primitive grains and wheat, used flint instruments, herded and hunted various animals and sometimes produced matted textiles of the simplest sort. Before 4000 BC the new farming techniques were being used in north Germany and Denmark. The same is true of Britain and northern France, though their contact probably came from southern France and from Iberia by sea.

In about 3500 BC two new dominant cultures spread westwards from central Europe. In the north, the so-called Funnel-beaker culture covered the area from Poland and Austria in the east to central Sweden and Holland in the west. These were the people who built the long dolmens or hunebedden of Holland, Germany and many of those in Denmark. One of their villages has been excavated near Oldenburg and this will be described in the chapter on Germany. These people did not bring the custom of megalithic building with them – it may be that their monuments were built after contacting and adopting a religion whose architectural technique was already prevalent in the British Isles and perhaps in Denmark.

At around the same period, another culture can be identified in the area from south Germany and Switzerland to Belgium; this is known as the Michelsberg culture, and it was probably responsible for the isolated menhirs erected over large parts of southern Germany. But it seems that these people did not have a religion which required the building of chambered mounds.

Yet another distinct group occupied southern Belgium and northern France slightly later – these people seem to have moved up from southern France and they are generally called the Sein-Oise-Marne or SOM culture. Wéris, the major megalithic monument in Belgium, is probably their work, as are many dolmens of the gallery-grave type in north France.

Well before 3000 BC big megalithic chambered mounds of various designs were being built by other peoples in Ireland, Great Britain and Brittany. During the following millennium these people started to build giant stone circles and alignments away from man-made mounds, with standing stones far larger than was necessary for astronomical studies.

The Beaker culture, which spread over much of Europe in the centuries following 2500 BC and gradually developed the use of bronze, may have grown from a cross-fertilization of the Michelsberg and Funnel-beaker talents and inventiveness. Another theory, however, has it that the new techniques originated in Spain and spread northwards (MacKie 1977). The early part of the Bronze Age was a wealthy period in Denmark, Brittany, much of the British Isles and most of Germany – but a time of poverty in the Netherlands and Belgium, which became a backwater of poor farmers without the metal ores.

The Beaker people established themselves strongly in Britain shortly before 2000 BC, where they seem to have taken up the megalithic ideas already developing independently in various parts of the islands; the great spread of the smaller stone circles associated with the study of astronomy occurred during the following centuries. Similarly, in Brittany the later megalith builders developed their own local forms, although these are linked to other parts of Europe by some shared architectural, decorative and functional characteristics. Brittany, if anywhere, was the meeting-point of northern and southern Europe and has been described at the beginning of this book.

In many parts of northern Europe, the dominance of the Beaker culture by 2000 BC and the increasing use of metal coincided with the end of building with the big stones – later monuments from the Low Countries northwards were apparently of earth and timber with some smaller stone chambers or cists. Where it had not already ceased, the building of megaliths ended when the climate of northern Europe became damp, cloudy and colder around 1500 BC.

Belgium today is grouped, in the minds of most European people, with the Low Countries in general. The east of the country is indeed fairly flat and the megalith builders do not seem to have found it attractive. But in the west of Belgium lie the Ardennes, an area of flowing hills with many steep slopes. Here, around Wéris, there is one of Europe's most evocative megalithic sites.

The earliest Neolithic finds in Belgium were from Omal, near Liège, to the north of Wéris. These remains were of early Danubian settlements and may well date from before 4000 BC. Halfway through the following millennium, the Michelsberg culture spread into north-eastern Belgium, and later than that the Seine-Oise-Marne culture fanned out from northern France into the Ardennes. Several dolmens and about a dozen isolated menhirs, probably of this period after 3000 BC, are known in the Ardennes – the best known menhir is the rugged Pierre-qui-tourne at Valaine-sur-Sambre in the province of Namur, although another at Bray stood 22 feet (nearly 7 metres) high until it was destroyed in the last century. The SOM culture lasted until the Beaker people overran it – it is possible that the menhirs date from Beaker times, but on the whole it seems that the Beaker folk in the Low Countries did not develop the possibilities of megaliths as they may have done in Brittany, the British Isles and elsewhere. Whoever built the various monuments at Wéris, it is hard to doubt that it was the most sacred megalithic centre between Brittany and Visbek in northern Germany.

Wéris is a pretty little village of no special distinction today. It lies five kilometres north of the town of Erezée, on one side of a prosperous valley in which several streams flow from springs only to disappear again beneath the earth. Three kilometres out of Erezée, the hamlets of Oppagne and Wénin are signposted to the left, and it is here that the remarkable Wéris, cross-country alignment starts. A few hundred metres beyond Wénin, three menhirs (known as the Oppagne menhirs) can be seen from the road in a field on the left.

55. Belgium. The three Oppagne menhirs which start the cross country alignment of monuments near Wéris near Erezée in the Ardennes. The tallest of the three is 8 feet (2.5 metres) high. The alignment is thought to date from the period between 3000 and 2500 BC.

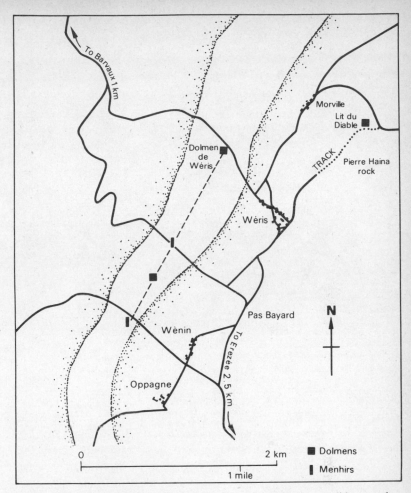

Fig. 23. Outline map of the two-kilometre long alignment and other megaliths around Wéris, near Erezée in eastern Belgium.

The Oppagne menhirs are a haunting group, standing close to an aged cherry tree of great height. Like all the nearby megaliths, they are of a pudding-stone which cracks off with fairly clean rectangular edges. The tallest of the three standing stones is some 8 feet (2.4 metres) tall. It has been suggested that they are fragments of one large menhir – for groups of three are rare – but anyone who has seen many standing stones will immediately recognize the twisted-top outline as a

56. The sunken dolmen of the gallery type provides the second point in the Wéris alignment. The three capstones have an overall length of 30 feet (9.2 metres).

favourite shape of the megalith builders. The line of the three acts as a baseline, as it were, at right angles to the extraordinary alignment that runs for over two kilometres north-north-east from here across the gently rolling fields. This alignment runs midway between the steeper slopes of the valley.

The next monument on the alignment lies about 600 metres farther north across the fields – the land is cultivated, but a farmtrack (which starts a little way back along the road towards Wènin) makes it possible to walk fairly close to the line. A small wood grows about forty metres to the right of the track after one has walked for a few minutes, and under these trees lies a massive half-buried dolmen of the type the French call an *allée couverte* – it is not marked on the local Belgian maps. It has a porthole in its entrance stone and is again of the local pudding-stone. When it was excavated, the chamber contained the remains of several human beings, animal bones and charcoal from a fire,

57. The single menhir of the Wéris alignment, re-erected on the edge of the field where it was found buried. The major Wéris dolmen, which continues the line, lies under the distant trees visible to the right of the menhir in this picture.

a broken flint axe and broken pottery of a coarse pre-Beaker sort (De Laet 1958, 107). There are signs of other excavations in the ground a few metres away from the dolmen.

Continuing 300 metres on the line north-north-east, a minor road crosses the alignment and a large menhir has been re-erected in the wall at the roadside. This menhir was found fallen and buried in the field nearby – its exact position was not recorded and this brings us to first dispute about Wéris. Paul de Saint-Hilaire has argued that the stone may have been positioned farther east when found – in that case, he believes, what seems a long alignment today was not a straight line at all but part of a mirror outline of the constellation Ursa Major, the Great Bear. Saint-Hilaire makes up the seven stars of the constellation from the four main monuments of the Wéris alignment, plus a domed stone known locally as Pas de Bou at Bouchaimont to the south, a spring at Morville to the north and a small dolmen called the Lit du Diable, which we shall mention shortly (Saint-Hilaire 1976, 18). The marking out of constellations on the earth, on a vast scale, 'as above, so below', is one of the most mysterious and awe-inspiring kinds of work left to us from remote times. The Glastonbury Zodiac is of course the best known of these. This imaginative interpretation has much interest and it reminds us of the cupmarks at Er Lannic near Carnac in a pattern-like Ursa Major (Le Rouzic 1930). But the present unique line of monuments across the fields at Wéris has equal fascination, for it has obvious similarities to less well-preserved lines of prehistoric sites across the countryside detected in England and in Germany.

The fourth structure in the alignment is over a kilometre beyond the re-erected menhir, under another group of trees. This is the Dolmen de Wéris itself, which can be reached by continuing along the farmtracks or by taking the road north-west out of Wéris village. It is a major dolmen by any standards, 36 feet (11 metres) long and with an enorous capstone. This structure stands above ground level, whereas the first dolmen in the alignment was apparently built at a level dug down into the soil. It is worth noting that both dolmens have entrances pointing along the alignment itself, which is reason to wonder what the significance was of the direction north-north-east. There is an obvious similarity to the dolmens of Corsica, some of which face along alignments on a much smaller scale, but these align due south. North-north-east is too northerly for the midsummer sunrise, so one is driven to conclude that the direction may have been decided by some magical importance attached to the lie of the valley. We do not know whether there were originally other megaliths in the alignment. Without the trees which now grow above the dolmens, the monuments would be visible from each other if there were one more marker between the Oppagne menhirs and the first dolmen. It is possible that the line was used in some way for observation or other rites. Saint-Hilaire points out that Ursa Major acted as near-Pole stars until 3100 BC, and the fixing of north was obviously an important piece of knowledge for travellers by night on sea or land.

The big Wéris dolmen makes a splendid end to the line of monu-

58. The Wéris dolmen itself, 36 feet (11 metres) in length. This is the last known monument in the long alignment, although a shattered pile of stones a few metres beyond it may have formed another menhir.

ments up the middle of the valley, though it is not quite the end – a few metres farther north along the line there are several broken stones which appear to be fallen menhirs, so the alignment may have finished with a row at right angles, as at Oppagne. Nor is the alignment the only important group of stones around Wéris. In the forested hills one kilometre north-east of the village, there is a small dolmen called Le Lit du Diable and almost above it on the hill an extraordinary outcrop of rock known as La Pierre Haina.

La Pierre Haina, which Saint-Hilaire translates from the Breton language as the 'rock of the ancestors', projects from the ground at an angle of 45° at the end of a spur which then falls sharply to the valley on three sides. It is of great size and rather menacing – it certainly looks as though it was partly man-carved to make it more impressive. One is inevitably reminded of Corsica again, where the great carved rock at Filitosa is in the same position on its spur and appears to have been the core of the sanctuary. The slight platform behind La Pierre Haina has not been excavated so it is not known whether there was any sort of cult enclosure there, but the local legends about the rock's magic powers are still strong. There was a tradition that Pierre Haina had to be whitewashed each year at the vernal equinox, and on this occasion all the people of the village would dance around the stone. This custom died out at the beginning of this century. According to one legend this rock closed a tunnel plunging to the centre of the earth. On certain evenings a mysterious being would lift the stone, and come out, roaming the countryside on his unknown tasks. When his work was done he would rest on the Lit du Diable till first cock-crow, when he would go back into his hole, carefully replacing the Pierre Haina as a stopper. Various versions of this story were told by local people during a visit to Wéris in 1975. If it was an object of veneration in megalithic times, it would explain why its surroundings contain so many monuments. None of the existing techniques can detect the earliest date at which La Pierre Haina may have been venerated, but the alignment of megaliths in the valley below probably dates from the period between 3000 and 2500 BC.

Two other sites in the Ardennes deserve mention here. Just south of Wéris is the hamlet called Pas Bayard. There is a stone of the same name in one of the streets there, in which is imprinted an outline like that of a gigantic hoof. Bayard is said to have been the horse of one of Charlemagne's generals who took a gigantic leap from this point to escape from enemies, according to one legend – another version is that the horse leapt from here to the stars where he now pulls the chariot of the Great Bear. The stone looks like a fair-sized capstone.

A good distance south-west of Wéris lies the village of Forrières, near Nassogne. A few hundred metres outside the village to the west, on a small road, there is a modern Calvary and above it on a spur the remains of a megalithic curiosity. Today on the slight platform there is nothing but six scattered stones, only one of which is even partly upright. In the middle of the nineteenth century, this monument was described as a miniature Stonehenge (De Laet 1958, 111) – it consisted of eighteen stones arranged as a circle of six trilithons, only one stone of which was missing. The longest stone on the small site is less than about 7 feet (2 metres) long and the surroundings are unsuitably steep for celestial observation. One might be inclined to dismiss the structure as one of the many megalithic follies put up in Europe a hundred years ago, but for one fact. The site itself is a classic one for the building of a megalithic monument, as described in the introduction to this book. The position above the steep slope of the spur, the way the hills are seen to wrap around behind it and the small valley which flows away before it are all features seen again and again when visiting megaliths. What the use of trilithons on such a small scale could be, remains a mystery.

The megalith builders almost always settled in hilly country, so it is not surprising that they did not take to most of what is now the Netherlands. In 5000 BC modern Holland was largely marshes or stretches of shallow sea not yet reclaimed. Yet a strip of very slightly higher and naturally drained land runs from the south up the eastern side of Holland towards Groningen in the north, and it is on this strip that the important Dutch megaliths are found. It is known as 'Oude Drenthe', old Drenthe, and is still reckoned by the rest of Holland to be a very traditional, conservative area with its own kind of huge deep roof, often thatched, on its houses and barns.

Early in the Neolithic period farmers of the culture which had spread from the east up the great Danube river settled in the south-east of the Netherlands a few centuries after 5000 BC. Traces of a village of built by these people lie under modern houses in the town of Geelen in Limburg province. The five Long Houses of Geelen were set informally and at odd angles to each other, though all five are orientated very roughly south-east to north-west – the largest of the houses is 105 feet (32 metres) long. The structures were of large timbers, with roofs and walls partly of wattle and daub. This and contemporary villages in Germany had no defences. These farmers built no megaliths and they simply appear to have died out after a few centuries – there seems to have been a considerable gap in time before the so-called Funnel-beaker farming culture arrived in the Netherlands, during which older hunter-gatherer communities continued their way of life.

It was these Funnel-beaker makers who moved along the strip of dry land 20 metres higher than the rest, up into the province of Drenthe in north-east Holland. Their origin is thought to have been in Poland or central Germany and it is believed that they flourished in the Netherlands from about 3400 until 2300 BC (De Laet 1958, 82-9, dates calibrated), when they appear to have declined into a poor province of

59. The Netherlands. A typical hunebed or long dolmen of the the province of Drenthe, in the north-east of the country. All the fifty-five surviving hunebedden are thought to date from between 3400 and 2300 B C. This example lies in the country east of the village of Borger; it is 25 feet (7.7 metres) long and the entrance faces south-east.

the more general Beaker culture developing at that time in surrounding countries. All the Dutch long dolmens, generally known in Holland as hunebedden (Huns' Beds), seem to have been built before the Beaker period proper and before the first appearance of bronze.

The Funnel-beaker culture had no megalith-building tradition of its own (De Laet 1958, 82) but contact with western European peoples outside Holland perhaps sparked their interest. All but one of the fifty-five surviving hunebedden in Holland (another thirty-two are recorded but destroyed) are in the province of Drenthe – outside that province the same people simply buried their dead in the ground. The reason for this was simply that the megalithic strip of Holland is a glacial moraine and big boulders are plentiful. Elsewhere there are hardly any suitable rocks. To the west of the strip the marshes ran to the sea, to the east there were marshes again for many kilometres until the next higher land in Germany is reached and the long dolmens become common again.

The greatest concentration of hunbedden in Drenthe is between the towns of Assen and Emmen, with fine monuments in the fields around Rolde, Gieten, Drouwen, Borger, Buinen, Odoorn and Emmen itself –

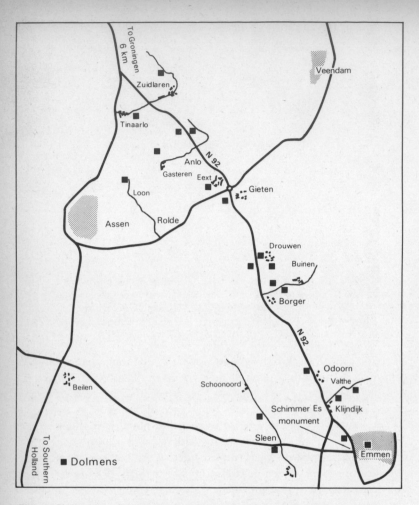

Fig. 24. Outline map of the area around Emmen and Assen in Drenthe province, north-east Holland, with the chief Hunebedden or long dolmens marked.

this is a good route to take when visiting them. The typical hunebed has a long chamber running approximately south-west to north-east and partly sunk into the soil, with a row of trilithons – two uprights roofed by a capstone – over it (there are no simple dolmens, that is with only one capstone, in Holland). The entrances are generally on the south-east and are sometimes emphasized by a trilithon of their own. The length of

60. The great hunebed on the north-west outskirts of Borger. It is about 80 feet (25 metres) long and its long chamber has ten capstones.

61. The short entrance passage, with a portal consisting of one trilithon, of the great Borger hunebed. The entrance faces south-east, towards the winter sunrise.

62. Interior of the long chamber of the large Borger hunebed, which runs from south-west to north-east. The chamber was originally considerably deeper, dug into the ground.

the monuments varies from over 70 feet (21 metres) to about 14 feet (4.3 metres), while there are as many as ten capstones along the ridge of the largest ones. Around many hunebedden there are signs of an oval or circular ring of smaller standing stones, called a kerb or revetment. It is believed that originally this kerb marked the bottom of a mound which sloped up to the monument but left the row of great capstones showing above. They must have been imposing presences in that form, though they are highly impressive in their present stripped state too – sometimes looking like great reptiles in the gentle Dutch countryside, often oddly disarming, like a child's drawing of a dinosaur.

The obvious function of the chambers inside the hunebedden was collective burial, although some single burials have been found in small ones. Most of them have been excavated and often contained several layers of human remains, sometimes paved over. The grave goods with the bones were usually pottery and broken flint implements. Much broken pottery has also been found outside the entrances to these long dolmens, confirming that there were ceremonies there too. This is not surprising, for the hunebedden are the only type of megalithic monument found in Holland – with one exception mentioned below – so that all these people's seasonal rituals probably took place there.

Some of the long dolmens on the journey from Assen to Emmen are quite difficult to find – inevitably much time will be spent going down the wrong track through the woods and heathland which abound in this area. The hunebedden at Rolde and the pair near the main road at Drouwen should not be missed. Approaching the end of the journey, an especially fine example can be seen in the northern outskirts of Borger. This tremendous dolmen is nearly 80 feet (24 metres) long and is of great beauty in its present clearing in the woods. The entrance is marked by a fine trilithon like a porch – the careful selection of almost matching capstones, rounded like tortoise-shells, was obviously of importance to the builders.

Emmen, where the concentration of megaliths ends, has several hunebedden around its outskirts. It also has another megalithic monument which is almost unique and the most impressive in Holland. This is the raised enclosure in the Schimmer Es fields, just across the road from the western edge of the town.

The Schimmer Es enclosure is a structure shaped almost like a ship, over 130 feet (40 metres) long, with two smallish chambers within its mass and a single standing stone rising slightly in the centre of its more pointed end. The raised earth platform is surrounded by powerful

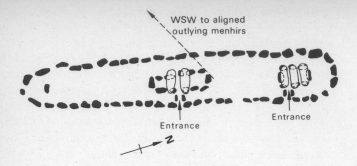

Fig. 25. Plan of the Schimmer Es raised enclosure, Emmen.

standing stones up to 6 feet (1.8 metres) high, with drystone walling between them. There is much similarity to the long raised quadrilaterals found in Germany and Denmark, while this structure also reminds one of the frontages of some English long barrows. The narrower end of the raised enclosure points just west of true south, and the chamber entrances in the side of the monument therefore face south of east, roughly in the direction of the winter sunrise, as is common in early megaliths. The chambers are very low as found today – presumably they were originally dug down into the ground. Several outlying standing stones can be seen in the pretty woods around the raised enclosure – these seem to indicate some astronomical purpose for the site, as well as obvious ritual and funerary uses. The outliers are all on the western side of the monument.

The age of the earliest hunebedden has been a subject of dispute. The evidence indicates that some of the hunebedden in the Netherlands and their equivalent long dolmens in Germany go back to about 3400 BC, as early as the dysser in Denmark (De Laet 1958, 86, dates calibrated). The pottery found during excavations of hunebedden has decoration limited to straight vertical and horizontal lines, and the twin circles, known as the double eye, which are often associated with the Great Goddess. It is probable that they were still being built until the Beaker culture ended the practice of collective burial in northern Europe generally. Here again we face the mystifying fact that in some areas (for example, the British Isles and Brittany) the arrival of the Beaker culture and of the first metal-working after 2500 BC seems to

63. The Schimmer Es raised enclosure, in the fields on the western edge of Emmen, at the south end of the hunebed area in Drenthe, Holland. The monument (whose length is 130 feet or 40 metres) is seen here from its narrower end, which points approximately south-south-west. The tallest stones can just be seen at the far end, as can the chambers (whose entrances face towards the winter sunrise). The design has obvious similarities to the aligned enclosures of Germany and Denmark, and perhaps to the long barrows of England. Like all those monuments, it probably dates from 3000 BC or earlier.

have stimulated important new types of megaliths – while in other places (such as the Netherlands, Belgium and even Iberia) the period seems to signal the end of megalithic development. It may be that the new culture took up the strongest interests already being followed in each part of Europe, or that it was only in areas where astronomical studies were highly developed that megalith building caught the fancy of the Beaker peoples.

Part of the explanation may lie in the fact that the Netherlands then became a cultural and technological backwater, still using flint implements for the most part, for many centuries during the Early Bronze and Beaker period in the surrounding countries. Contemporary Brittany, Wessex and Germany produced great splendours at this time, but the Low Countries had none of the important metal ores and their people deteriorated into groups of poor farmers. Their pottery and decoration became primitive. Bronze objects were rare. They did produce several lesser versions of the Schimmer Es raised enclosure; these have been found at Weerdinge in Drenthe, in Dutch Limburg and – outside Holland – near Mont de l'Enclus in Flanders and near Aachen in Germany. But most of the building that was done in Holland was of timber rather than of stone. Roadways of around 2000 BC, with surfaces of tree-trunks laid from side to side, were built across the marshes. Four solid wooden wheels of the same period have been found in Drenthe (Piggott 1973, 94). The burial-chambers were almost always of wood too. At Zeijen in Drenthe, the round barrow numbered 75 on the Noordse Veld had two circles of upright tree-trunks around it and an approach avenue some 150 feet (46 metres) long running from the south-east, formed by two rows of wooden posts. The post-holes, which are all that remain of this vanished monument, have yet to be analysed to see whether it may have had an astronomical function. If so, that might be at least one sign of developing scientific and religious activity among these poverty-stricken farmers before another period of prosperity started for them by 1000 BC.

10 Germany – Visbek

Modern Germany, east and west, covers a very large part of northern central Europe. On the west, the river Rhine has traditionally provided its border, while the Baltic to the north and the Alps to the south are natural boundaries. But on the east it has no geographical feature to define its limits and the states which composed Germany, until its unification a century ago, expanded and contracted to the east many times during written history. Numerous invasions from the east are recorded and many more have left their traces from prehistory for archaeologists to analyse. With this background, it is hardly surprising that the country does not show a consistent pattern of megaliths throughout. A glance at the map of Europe at the beginning of this book will show that dolmens, or megalithic chambered mounds, are found throughout the northern part of Germany – as far south as the Ruhr, Kassel on the river Weser and Halle on the river Saale – while they were built eastwards as far as Stettin on the Baltic coast and beyond into Poland. The map accompanying this chapter charts the distribution of menhirs – single standing stones – and shows that they were erected in large areas of south-western and central Germany, almost precisely south of the line where the dolmens cease.

As in Holland, the first farmers seem to have arrived in Germany two or three centuries after 5000 BC, having spread up the river Danube from the east. These Danubian people do not seem to have built megaliths.

Around 3500 BC the so-called Michelsburg culture spread throughout southern Germany as far as modern Belgium and Luxembourg. It is very rarely possible to date solitary menhirs, but it was presumably these people or the Beaker culture which followed them after 2500 BC that erected the standing stones in south Germany. On the whole it seems more likely that it was the earlier people that were responsible, for the characteristic products of the Beaker people have been found

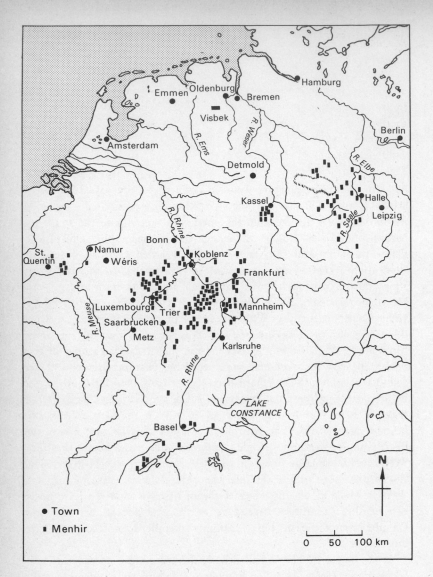

Fig. 26. Outline map of central and southern Germany, showing the distribution of menhirs in the countryside and the positions of other megalithic sites mentioned in this book.

only in well-defined areas (Piggott 1965 and 1973, 101) and these do not coincide for the most part with the menhirs recorded by German scholars, as shown on our map.

The purpose of these menhirs is obscure. They exist in wide patches of country north of Trier, west and north of Mannheim, south and thinly along a line north-north-east of Frankfurt, south of Kassel and then over a wide area bordered on the east by Halle and Leipzig. They may have been objects of veneration in themselves or perhaps fore-sights for astronomical observations. One man, the clergyman Wilhelm Teudt in the 1920s, saw them as part of a system of straight lines, like the leys traced in England during the same decade, linking ancient German sacred sites.

Near Detmold in Lower Saxony, seventy-five kilometres north-west of Kassel, there are some gigantic needles of rock, called Die Externsteine, in the Teutoburger Wald. The top of one of these rock pinnacles has a chamber carved within its mass. The chamber has long been used as a chapel, but it is thought to be much older than Christianity. One wall of the chamber has a round window in it, while there is a niche in the opposite rock wall. From the centre of that niche an observer can see the moon rise in its most northerly position through the circular window, while from the left-hand side in the niche the midsummer sunrise can be seen. The age of the chamber has not been proved, but Teudt and others believed that it was an observatory from megalithic times – certainly no later culture in northern Europe until our own would be likely to go to great trouble to construct such a celestial labora-tory. Teudt also believed that the Externsteine rocks and other monu-ments in the Teutoburger woods were the heartland of prehistoric Ger-many – from this place he charted straight lines going out across the country, cutting through hermitages, old churches, chapels, standing stones, towers, crosses and moots. These were the places of ancient festivals, he wrote, where people gathered to watch the sun or moon rise beyond further markers erected on the horizon – thus creating other straight lines to be extended until the land was bound by a net-work of them (Teudt 1929; Michell 1977). Certainly, on the side of the Externsteine rocks there is a fine medieval carving which represents Charlemagne trampling down the ancient tree of life (Irmensul or Ygdrasil) to lift Christ down from the cross – this is clearly referring to the suppression of an earlier religion by Christianity, the stamping out of an older wisdom.

There is another site in Germany that may reasonably claim to be the

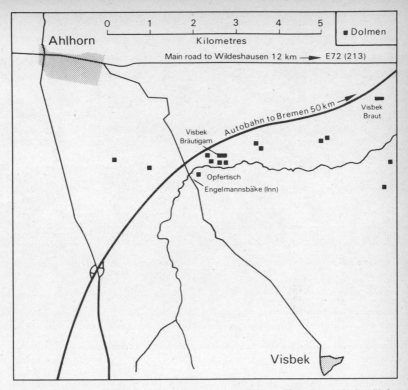

Fig. 27. Outline map of the area around Visbek in north-west Germany with the chief megalithic monuments marked.

ancient sacred centre of the north, however. This is the great group of megaliths near Visbek, fifty kilometres west of Bremen. This part of Germany has a great many long dolmens (called in Germany a Steingrab or Hünengrab, i.e. Huns' Grave). These are of the same type as the hunebed which is found in northern Holland – the Funnel-beaker people seem to have occupied all the cultivable land in this part of Europe between 3400 and 2300 BC. The absence of megaliths along the north–south Ems river seems to have been for the simple reason that

64. Germany. The Visbek Bride (Visbeker Braut) aligned enclosure, in the forests west of Bremen. The quadrilateral, which is 260 feet (80 metres) long, points from the four great stones at the far end and narrows towards the north-east. It is believed that it was built in the centuries around 3000 BC and may have enclosed an earth platform like the Schimmer Es monument in Holland. There is a megalithic chamber at the far end of the enclosure, now without a capstone.

167

65. Dolmen beside the forest path approaching the Visbek Bridegroom.

the slight valley was all marshes between two areas of slightly higher ground, now in Holland and Germany respectively.

Before describing the Visbek megaliths, it is interesting to look at the evidence about the people who built them. To the north of Visbek, a village of the Funnel-beaker culture dating from before 2500 BC has been excavated at Dümmerlohausen, Oldenburg. It consisted of more than forty rectangular houses, with timber frames and walls of clay-daubed wattle, and with planked floors. Almost all the houses had a porch and two rooms inside, each room of about 10 × 6 feet (3 × 1.8 metres). The people were farmers of cattle, sheep and pigs as well as growing wheat, barley and spelt. They ate apples, raspberries and hazel-nuts and they fished and hunted for deer, wild boar, beavers, wolves and bears. They had dogs and horses. The village was surrounded by a palisade of tree-trunks.

Doubtless many such villages existed in northern Germany. Each would probably have its own long dolmen, with its great capstones showing above the mound, as its temple for seasonal religious ceremonies and for collective burials. But the grand enclosures at Visbek surely formed a centre for the most special festivals for people from a wide area, as Avebury probably did in England.

A number of such enclosures exist in north Germany, but those known as the Visbeker Braut und Bräutigam (Bride and Bridegroom) are the largest and are surrounded by many long dolmens. The country is thickly wooded today, but would have been cleared farmland in the years rather before 3000 BC when the enclosures were probably built. The group is close to the autobahn from Bremen to Osnabruck, which should be left by the exit for Wildeshausen and Ahlhorn. Turning left on the main road towards Ahlhorn, the Visbeker Braut is soon signposted down a track to the left – this runs under the autobahn and the monument is a short distance beyond that among the forest trees on the right. Later, to reach the Visbeker Bräutigam, continue on the main road towards Ahlhorn, turn left at Sandhorn onto a minor road which winds back across the autobahn again and park at a large country inn on the left called the Engelmannsbäker – a path is then signposted through the forest. It is wise to avoid the rough forest tracks between the two monuments if you are travelling by car.

The Visbeker Braut is an extraordinarily beautiful long quadrilateral enclosure in a forest clearing. It is 260 feet (80 metres) long and 23 feet (7 metres) wide at its broader end – for it is not rectangular. Aligned south-west to north-east, the south-west end is marked by four large standing stones about 7 feet (2 metres) high. Two lines of stones run away from this end, the granite rocks becoming smaller and the enclosure narrowing so that the effect is like a truncated arrowhead pointing north-east. That is roughly towards the midsummer sunrise, but the possibility of a solar or astronomical function has not yet been analysed. The arrangement is like that of the Carnac alignments, but on a smaller scale. At the far end the alignments are terminated by two larger standing stones but there are no stones between these. In the middle of the enclosure, towards the broader end, there is a chamber of slabs sunk into the earth – doubtless this had capstones originally and was used for burials, at least that is the case in other enclosures of this general type from the Netherlands to Denmark. Again, the megalith builders often built their burial-places close to, or even within, their sanctuaries, and rituals for the living surely gained in 'mana' from the continuity ensured by the presence of the dead.

The Visbeker Bräutigam is even larger than the Braut. Leaving the Engelmannsbäker inn, there is a dolmen with a large flat capstone on

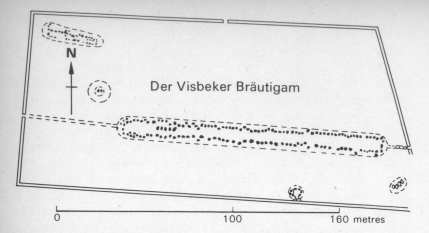

N

Der Visbeker Bräutigam

0   100   160 metres

Fig. 28. Plan of the Visbek Bridegroom aligned quadrilateral and its surrounding dolmens.

the right of the path. A bridge crosses a stream, and the path continues through the forest. The enormous enclosure appears after a few minutes, closely surrounded by the trees. The standing stone rows here and at the Braut may originally have lined a raised platform of earth, as at similar monuments in Holland and Denmark. The Braütigam is 354 feet (108 metres) long and 33 feet (10 metres) wide – it is aligned almost exactly east–west. The end stones are up to 8 feet (2.4 metres) high in the east and 4 feet 6 inches (1.4 metres) in the west. Like the Braut, it has a large sunken stone chamber in its middle, towards the western end in this case, with five big capstones intact. But unlike the Bride, the Bridegroom does not taper at one end. It stands four-square, east–west – presumably calculated by the equinox sunrise or sunset as these people probably had no compass. The symbolism of this is a matter for speculation. East–west has been interpreted as symbolizing stability and permanence, and even as referring to the creation itself, in temples in many parts of the world. On the other hand, the long shapes of the great enclosures seem to be pointing, perhaps towards a significant place on the horizon. It may be that we should imagine crowds from miles around gathering in and about the Braut for ceremonies involving the sunrise at the summer solstice, and at the Bräutigam to mark the equinox. Of course, the trees block the views of the horizon today and it is difficult to see even the lie of the rolling country around.

66. The Visbek Bridegroom (Visbeker Bräutigam) aligned enclosure, west of Bremen. This quadrilateral is 354 feet (110 metres) long and points east–west, without narrowing at either end. Seen here from the west, the largest standing stones are at the far end, while the capstoned chamber was built (unusually) towards the west. As with the Bride, the stones may have enclosed an earth platform when it was built in about 3000 BC.

67. Hünnegrab or long dolmen, of a type similar to the Hunebedden of Holland, about a hundred yards north-west of the Visbek Bridegroom. The oval ring of stones around the long chamber probably acted as a kerb for a low mound which would leave the row of boulder capstones exposed along its ridge.

The Bräutigam lacks the grace and beauty of the other enclosure, but has such an impressively powerful presence of its own that one can understand the imaginative German antiquary who gave the two their present names. Among the trees around the Bräutigam there are four other dolmens. Towards the north-west there is a round barrow with only its capstone visible and, beyond it, a long dolmen similar to the Dutch hunebedden with an elliptical kerb or revetment around it. Beyond the south-east corner of the enclosure there is a sunken dolmen with four enormous capstones perched at ground level, and another oval monument. Today the whole complex is romantically suggestive of the deep shadows of Teutonic legend. Without the woods the feeling would be very different, but to come to such a centre on great feast days must have been a moving experience for Neolithic farmers who had travelled far across the cleared land from their outlying villages.

68. Sunken hünnegrab south-east of the Visbek Bridegroom. This and other dolmens
around the Visbek sanctuary date from the years of
the Funnel-beaker culture, probably between 3000 and 2300 BC.

11   Denmark

Throughout northern Europe grand megalithic monuments are set in surroundings of lyrical beauty, rolling hills of no great size, rather than dramatic mountains or completely flat plains. One reason for settling in such places was that they offered well-drained farmland with good soil at the time. But this can also be expressed as an intentional choice of land where nature is in harmony with man – a feeling that one gets again and again at megalithic sites, even those which have turned into peat-covered moors since the weather deteriorated around 1500 BC. Denmark is full of such blessed countryside – there are some flat areas, but most of it has fairly low hills and valleys of great charm. The country also has many islands and a long coastline, and the megalith builders found both these features attractive. Denmark has a denser distribution of megaliths than any other country. Its area is small, yet it has 3500 recorded dolmens of several types, compared with 5000 in the much larger area of France and 2000 in the British Isles (Piggott 1965 and 1973, 60). It does not, however, have the variety of megalithic structures of those countries – the stone circles are only those around dolmens, not of the open type of which the British Isles have 900 examples. There are no true menhirs.

Human beings reappeared in Denmark soon after the Ice Age drew back towards the north. The known Mesolithic cultures include the Maglemosian around 8000 BC and the Ertebølle, which produced crude pottery a couple of thousand years later. The first farmers probably arrived from the Danube basin via Germany a little before 4000 BC, bringing wheat and barley as well as cattle, sheep and goats (Dyer 1972, 8. Dates given by authorities such as Munksgaard 1970 must be corrected to allow for subsequent discoveries and radiocarbon calibration). They made fine flint tools and low mounds to bury their dead, but they did not build megaliths. Earlier communities continued with their own hunting way of life after the farmers started to clear the forests.

Fig. 29. Outline map of Denmark showing the megalithic sites mentioned in this book.

The earliest megaliths in Denmark probably date from around 3400 BC. It is not clear whether all the monuments of this time were the work of one culture. The so-called round dolmens – with four or more supporting stones and a big capstone in a stone-kerbed mound – seem to have been the first to develop. But shortly afterwards, long barrows too appeared all over the country. The two types often occur close together and, as Elisabeth Munksgaard has pointed out, one or other can

69. Denmark. Part of the sacred centre at Tustrup on the Djursland peninsular, Jutland. The concentric rings of the great round dolmen seen from above the entrance (which faces south–east) to the mound of the passage grave. The Tustrup site has yielded a calibrated radiocarbon date of 3050 BC.

be found in almost every parish of Denmark. They were, of course, temples as well as tombs, as we shall see below. Later, different types of dolmen evolved, but there seems to be no evidence that either early design was the work of anyone but the same Funnel-beaker culture that built similar structures, with local differences, in northern Germany and Holland. All domens, chambered mounds or barrows are known by the general name *dysser* in Danish.

In Denmark the Funnel-beaker people lived in Long Houses of up to 200 feet (61 metres) in length, subdivided into many rooms – the classic example was found at Troldebjerg, with a variety of round huts around it. The structure of these houses was a frame of stout timber posts, infilled with wattle and daub. The megalith builders farmed the same crops and animals as the earlier farmers, but added pigs to the stock. They hunted deer, elk, wolf and bear, and seem to have eaten them all as well as using their skins for clothing. They cultivated apples and perhaps raspberries as well. They used flint implements and made ornaments of amber to adorn themselves. Their dead were buried collectively, one over another, in the dolmens – the Paeregaard dolmen on a clifftop in Langeland island contained only twenty skeletons, but their dates were spread over 1000 years. Other dolmens contained the bones of over a hundred human-beings. Their way of life, and death, spread from Denmark to the southern parts of Sweden and Norway.

The entrances to early dolmens in Denmark were blocked after each burial, so that other rites could only have taken place outside. Around 3000 BC a new design, like the passage graves elsewhere in Europe, was introduced. In these the entrance to the passage and chamber was usually left open, but even then the main non-funerary ceremonies seem to have taken place outside. At the Grønhøj chambered mound near Horsens in Jutland, over 7000 pottery shards were found piled in a layer a foot (0.3 metre) thick outside the entrance. Among these, there were twenty unbroken pots of 3000 BC. The mound and its entrance is surrounded by a kerb of standing stones; fragments of pottery were discovered on both sides, and even on top, of several of these surrounding stones. Some of the pieces of pottery from different sides of a stone could be reconstructed into a single pot. This patient piece of detective work has established with reasonable certainty that these shards had not simply been cleared out of the chamber to make more room. They were the legacy of rites performed outside the mound which involved smashing pots, perhaps containing libations, on the rocks. Most Danish dolmens' entrances face roughly south-east, to-

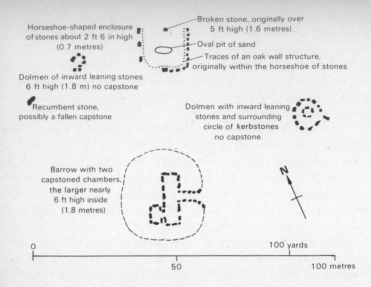

Fig. 30. Sketch plan of the megalithic site at Tustrup, on Djursland peninsular in Jutland, Denmark.

wards the winter sunrise.

There are so many megalithic monuments in Denmark that only some of the major typical or exceptional sites can be mentioned here. On the mainland, Jutland, the best site on the west coast is at Ølstrup, where there are three raised enclosures or long dysser and one round one on a hilltop (these long dysser as a type will be described in detail further on, with the major example on Møn island). In north Jutland, the well-known Troldkirken (the Trolls' Church) is a long dysser on top of a spur of land thirteen kilometres west of Aalborg – its kerbing of forty-eight stones, up to 6 feet 6 inches (2 metres) high, is 324 feet 9 inches (90 metres) long and surrounds a big polygonal chamber. Farther south is the Spanskhøj (the Spanish mound, literally) near Hannerup, a big barrow covering two round chambers of the passage-grave sort. East of the Spanskhøj lies the Djursland peninsula projecting into the Baltic sea, with two major sites which we shall describe in more detail.

Tustrup, in the north of Djursland, is arguably the most impressive group of megaliths in Denmark (though there are much later Iron Age and Viking sites which are more dramatic). It is in a remote part of the country, not far inland from a coast which today seems to exist only for the summer holiday season. A minor road runs from the village of Vivild to that of Tustrup. About halfway between the two, there is a small signpost on the south or right-hand side of the road, saying Stendyssene (Stone Dolmens, roughly translated) and pointing along a path. The path runs a few hundred metres down into a valley and up on to a broad hilltop, where the megaliths stand. Around the horizon there are higher hills to the west and the south, lower hills elsewhere. There are many woods and the country is gentle and rolling.

The layout of the group is shown in the accompanying diagram. Approaching from the north-west, the first structure reached is an oval or polygonal dolmen whose five orthostats lean inwards. The capstone is missing – it may be the flat stone which lies in the heather a few metres away. From this point it can be seen that this first dolmen, together with a large chambered mound and an encircled round dolmen, lie in a curve at a respectful distance around one side of a U-plan setting of small stones, which forms the heart of the sanctuary. The chambered mound is in fact a major example of the Danish type of passage grave, with two big chambers inside its covering, while the ring-kerbed round dolmen (again, its capstone is missing) is another classic among Danish megaliths. Their entrances face south-east. Both are of considerable grandeur, but it is the least impressive monument, the U-shaped enclosure, which holds the key to the site.

This enclosure, whose open side faces rather north of north-east, is often called a mortuary house by archaeologists. In fact, it is not known whether the complex rites which evidently took place there were necessarily connected with funerals. The horseshoe of standing stones, which are only about 2 feet 6 inches (0.7 metre) high, originally stood outside a wall of oak tree-trunks of unknown height. In the centre of the open side of the enclosure there is a standing stone – it is broken now, but from the two pieces archaeologists reckon that it originally stood over 5 feet (1.6 metres) high and was aligned towards the midsummer sunrise. The space within the enclosure (it is not clear whether it was roofed) measures over 16 feet (5 metres) by 18 feet (5.5 metres). In the centre of this space an oval pit full of sand was found. On either side of this pit, roughly on the east and on the west of it, there were groups of pots in the ground when it was excavated – these included six funnel-beakers, seventeen bowls of various sorts (one apparently designed to be suspended) and eight small ladles.

The Tustrup ritual enclosure was built shortly before 3000 BC,

70. The concentric dolmen at Tustrup – the capstone is missing. Beyond it lies the mound and entrance of the passage grave, while the ritual enclosure and the other dolmen are to the right, out of the picture.

according to calibrated radiocarbon datings taken from the charred wood of its oak walls, for the structure seems to have burned down at some stage. This suggests that fire may have played some part in the rites, but cremation of human remains was not introduced in Denmark until much later. The standing stone aligned from the oval pit of sand towards the midsummer sunrise seems to hint at dawn rituals involving libations contained in the pots and poured or burned on the sand. It has been suggested that the dead may have been kept in the enclosure during funeral rites before the body was placed in one of the burial-chambers nearby, but there is nothing to prove that. Whatever the ceremonies were, we can imagine those taking part moving around the great group of megalithic monuments in seasonal rites that concerned the sun or the moon or the balancing of nature's forces for the benefit of the land and mankind.

Apart from Tustrup, Djursland also has a considerable group of dolmens and mounds at its southern side, on a smaller projection of land called the Mols peninsula. The centrepiece of these remains is the Knebel round dolmen, often called the Paaskaer Stenhus, which is one of the finest encircled dolmens in any country. Its surrounding circle consists of twenty-three massive granite stones – of the rounded boulder shape usual in Denmark, rather than the slab type common in the British Isles. Two stones at east and west are markedly red in colour. From the west side of the stone circle – which originally enclosed a mound – two more stones provide a short passage into the dolmen itself, which is 7 feet (2.1 metres) high with a big round-topped capstone. But the siting of the Knebel dolmen is of even more interest than its architectural splendour. It stands on a small hillock at the top end of a valley whose hills wrap around behind it on three sides, while the valley runs down to the sea on the fourth side, leaving the horizon open. This is one of the clearest examples of the typical siting of megaliths so that the landscape falls in such a pattern around them, as described in the introduction to this book, because Neolithic man found a harmony of earth and sky at these places.

There are many other Neolithic sites in Jutland, but important examples of megalithic design also exist in the six largest islands which make up the rest of Denmark. On Zealand, the island on which Copenhagen is built, the Juliane Høj at Neder Draaby is a curiosity, for the barrow was restored with Classical detailing by the Crown Prince of Denmark in 1776. There is also a notable long dysser at Daempegaard, with two chambers enclosed by a rectangular mound. At Kirke Stillinge, eight kilometres north-west of Slagelse, there is a long dysser named Breddyssen beside a farm called Ølandsgaarden. The mound is in bad condition, but the chief point of interest is the carving of two ships, with cupmarks around them, which can be seen on the capstone of the western chamber – the carvings were perhaps added during the early Bronze Age, when most cupmarks were done.

71. Kong Asgers Høj, on the island of Møn, Denmark. One of the best preserved
mounds of the passage grave type. Again the entrance faces towards the winter sunrise.
Danish archaeologists have established that rites were performed outside the entrances
to such mounds as well as within.

On the island of Funen there is a barrow containing a particularly
large and tall passage grave chamber at Maarhøj, between Martofte
and Snave. The raised enclosure or long dysser at Lindeskov will be
dealt with below.

Langeland contains the clifftop Paeregaard dolmen already mentioned and two of the long dysser. To consider these great monuments more closely the place to start is the island of Møn.

Møn is smaller than the other islands mentioned here, but its western end is almost crowded with megalithic structures. At Jordehøj
there is a passage grave whose chamber narrows in the middle like
an hourglass. At Klekkendehøj the passage grave was constructed
uniquely with a wall across its centre to provide two chambers in one
structure. The most famous of these Møn passage graves is Kong
Asgers Høj, near the sea facing across to Zealand. Its mound and 33-
feet (10-metres) long chamber are remarkably complete. But it is the
Grønjaegers Høj that is the great reward for the journey to Møn.

72. The Grønjaegers Høj raised enclosure, on the island of Møn. The enclosure, one of the two largest in Denmark is 331 feet (102 metres) long and is aligned east–west. In these and other respects it resembles the West Kennet long barrow in England.

Long 'dolmens' of various sorts are common enough in northern Europe, but in a few places they developed into more ambitious sanctuaries – the enclosures mentioned earlier in this book at Emmen in Holland and at Visbek in Germany show a similar design development to the raised and aligned enclosures or long dysser of Denmark. In all of these countries there are one or more chambers within each enclosure, and human remains have been found in many of these. There is always a line of particularly tall stones across one end of the alignment, as if this were a baseline and the monument were pointing away from it. The direction in which they point, however, varies greatly. The Schimmer Es enclosure at Emmen points almost south, the Visbek Braut points north-east, the Bräutigam points just about due west (unless some even larger stones have disappeared from its western end) and the Grønjaegers Høj points due east.

Long barrows in other countries may also be related to these raised enclosures. There are many in Scotland, Wales and England (the famous West Kennet long barrow points east-west). Others are found in France – for example, the gallery-chambered Kerlescan long barrow, near Carnac, also points east–west. The details of all these monuments vary, but the architectural links are obvious. Their religious uses, apart from burials, were surely linked too.

The Grønjaegers Høj (the Green Huntsman's Mound) stands beside a farm within sight across the fields of the lovely Fanefjord pilgrimage church. The country is low and very gently undulating. It is best approached from the north along the edge of the fields between the dysser and the road (though there is a farmtrack for pedestrians from a car-park on the road to the west of the monument). From the north, the full extent of the long side of the enclosure can be seen under the trees which grow on top of it. It is 331 feet (101 metres) long; both sides of its quadrilateral mound are supported by long alignments of man-height standing stones and drystone walling between these 134 upright slabs. It is a true rectangle, 33 feet (10 metres) wide at each end – for comparison the Visbek Bräutigam is 354 feet (108 metres) long and also 33 feet (10 metres) wide, and both are aligned east–west although apparently pointing in opposite directions.

Between the avenue of stones, the trees form another avenue at a higher level along the top of the Grønjaegers Høj. Three great standing stones at the western end rise well above the level of the platform. A few metres along its central line, an enormous boulder forms the capstone of a chamber hidden in the ground below. Then the grass-

73. The boulder capstone of the chamber and, beyond, the three tall stones at the western end of the Grønjaegers Høj. Dating from the centuries around 3000 BC, these Danish monuments resemble similar aligned structures in the Netherlands, Germany and England.

covered enclosure runs away to the east under the trees, passing two more chambers – small and uncovered – along its route, and ends with a revetment of low stones just before the farm. The trees on top of the enclosure may offend purists, but they add to the enchantment of the great sanctuary.

Some students of Danish megaliths have expressed the view that such platforms are no more than rectangular mounds erected around a dolmen, but this is unconvincing. Again, tombs were clearly appropriate features, in the minds of the megalith builders, of their sanctuaries for seasonal and other rites of all kinds. We cannot be too far wrong if we imagine gatherings of people on these long platforms, observing festivals to contact the deities of nature. It remains to be seen whether there is any sign of scientific observations of the skies from such monuments.

The aligned and raised enclosures, which were built in all the countries occupied by the Funnel-beaker people between about 3400 and 2500 BC, are found most frequently in Denmark. We shall mention only a few of them here. Apart from the Grønjaegers Høj, there is a smaller one at Møn at Idalund (164 feet or 50 metres long). On the large island of Zealand, there is an example at Daempegaard, and on Lolland the fine Radsted long dysser is 262 feet (80 metres) long. There are two on Langeland – the impeccably restored one at Tryggelev Mark and the smaller Kong Humbles Grav (180 feet or 55 metres). There are many of various sizes on the mainland of Jutland, but the largest of all is about a kilometre north of the village of Lindeskov, west of Ørboek, on the island of Funen. This raised enclosure is no less than 546 feet (166 metres) long, with 126 standing stones along its sides and one small chamber within it.

It appears that no new megalithic chambered monuments were built in Denmark after about 2500 BC. The Funnel-beaker culture survived the incursions and settlements of an aggressive race of eastern warriors generally called the Battleaxe people around 2800 BC. But at the time when the wider Beaker culture started to spread through southern and central Europe later in that millennium, the people in Denmark started to adopt the foreign custom of single burial. By 2000 BC, most burials were in small stone cists, pointing north–south in Jutland and east–west in Zealand, although the old collective chambers were used as late as this in a few areas.

Neolithic men and women in Denmark were moving into a very different and less kindly age. The first imported metal objects appeared soon after 2500 BC, but it was 600 years later before local metal craftsmanship started in Denmark. The people traded their products for metal ores, and fine implements and ornaments of bronze or gold were made. Prosperity perhaps made up in part for the new violence of the age. The round barrow burials in hollowed tree-trunks adopted by some people around 1800 BC have preserved human bodies and clothing in extraordinarily good condition and many of these finds can be seen in the National Museum in Copenhagen. A blond man found at Muldbjerg in Jutland was 5 feet 4 inches (1.62 metres) tall and wore a calf-length robe which was fastened over one shoulder with a bronze brooch. Over the robe, he wore a dark cloak of much the same length, while his head was covered with a thick woolly round hat. A young woman discovered at Egteved wore a thinner robe with a golden stomacher around it. The clothes were of wool, which has lasted best, but there were also traces of vegetable fibres in the materials. The people of this relatively prosperous age did not build any megaliths, but there is evidence that some of them used the old sanctuaries for their religious ceremonies and seasonal festivals – bronze objects have been found at the sites and the cupmarks and other carvings of sunwheels and ships on the great stones are thought to date from this later period. And from this time, or perhaps going back to Neolithic days, the famous Haervejen road provided a route from near the north to the south of Jutland – like the Ridgeway in England, it can still be traced and used.

As in France and Germany, the megaliths of the British Isles were built by a number of different cultures whose territories did not coincide with today's boundaries. The first farming settlements in the islands go back before 4000 BC. The new agricultural techniques may have arrived first in western England or in Ireland – the enclosure at Knockiveagh in Ireland has been dated at 3700 BC and Maumbury Rings in England only a hundred years later. After that the customs of building chambered mounds and of collective burials spread widely and in the following 2000 years the islands developed more different kinds of megalithic monument than any other part of Europe. The forms of dolmen chamber found – within or without mounds and cairns – offer a rich study in themselves. The earthworks flung up at the time are titanic in scale and vary from henges to hillocks, from barrows to 'cursus' avenues across the countryside. Menhirs of all sizes and shapes are plotted across the countryside, sometimes forming long lines over the moors. Even more evocatively, hundreds of circles of standing stones ranging from the vast Avebury and Stonehenge to many a few metres across, are found in all the western and northern parts of Britain and most of Ireland. That distribution is fairly typical of the British megaliths as a whole – only in East Anglia and the Midlands of England and in the centre of Ireland, the most inland areas and the fen or bog counties, are they absent.

As we have noted before, the megalith builders loved the sea and islands. In the British Isles not only did they populate the coastal areas most thickly – Rollright, Avebury and Stonehenge are exceptionally far from the sea – but some of the greatest structures are on quite small islands. Orkney, the group of nearly seventy islands partly visible from the north coast of Scotland, was the leading example of a miniature society of the period. Chambered monuments (often called cairns in Scotland) exist on at least four of the smaller islands – including the chamber carved into the solid rock of a large boulder called the Dwarfie Stane or Stone, on Hoy island – and these probably served as sanctuaries for the smaller groups of people on each. Orkney is, in political terms, part of the United Kingdom today, but the Orcadians still think of themselves as a separate people. When they talk of Mainland, they mean the largest of their own islands – not the mainland of Scotland.

Fig. 31. Outline map of the British Isles, indicating the distribution of stone circles, the concentrations of dolmens or chambered mounds and cairns, and naming some of the most important sites of various types.

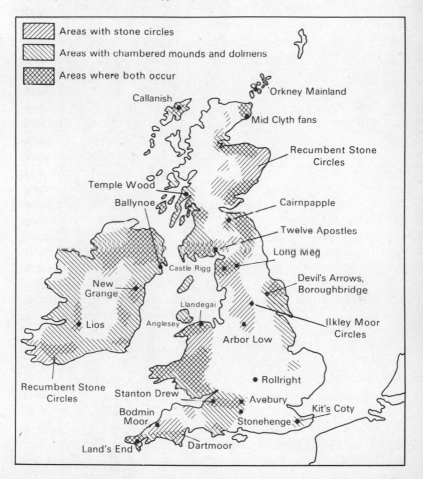

74. Orkney, Mainland island. View southwards over the Stenness landscape from near the vanished Ring of Bookan. The stones of the Ring of Brodgar can be seen in profile against the right-hand loch, while the Stenness ring lies just beyond the spit of land between the two lochs. The mound of Maes Howe is beyond the water to the left.

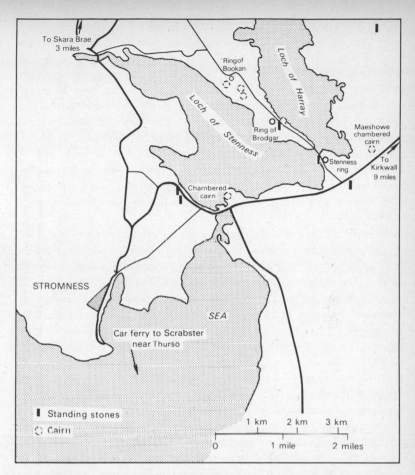

Fig. 32. Outline map of part of Orkney Mainland island, showing the megalithic centre around Stenness.

The earliest dated farming settlement on Orkney is Knap of Howar on Papa Westray island. Calibrated radiocarbon dates as early as 3500 BC have been obtained from the two stone dwellings here, while the latest date was 3100 BC. One house has an interior measuring 34 feet × 15 feet (9.7 × 4.8 metres) divided into two rooms, while the other is slightly smaller and has three rooms. Both have massively thick stone walls. The houses had a low bench of stone, hearths, cupboards in the walls and workbenches of both stone and wood. The people had grain, but most of the remains of food in the midden dumped around the houses pointed to a diet of shellfish, beef, mutton, pork and venison. They did not weave cloth, but the implements hint at clothes of furs and leather, quite finely stitched. The early pottery was crude, but it soon developed into the decorated type known as Unstan. There is an elongated mound on the nearby islet called Holm of Papa Westray, which contains a narrow chamber 70 feet (21.4 metres) long with no less than twelve small cells opening off it. The Neolithic carvings (rare in Orkney) like pairs of eyes and eyebrows, above one cell entrance of this monument, are motifs usually associated with worship of the Mother Goddess. It is possible that Papa Westray was the first settlement and sanctuary of the Orkney farmers, for the soil is unusually rich, though very early sites in other islands may remain unknown as yet.

If Papa Westray was the first centre, its importance probably declined around 3000 BC when the chambered mounds, individual standing stones and stone circles started to grow up at Stenness, which is close to the main road from Stromness to Kirkwall on Orkney Mainland. This is one of the greatest concentrations of big megalithic structures anywhere in Europe, and its surroundings are of outstanding beauty. With the exception of the mountains on Hoy, all the Orkney islands have soft green countryside of low hills which rise occasionally to higher, but still rounded, ridges. Stenness lies in a wide bowl with such ridges around much of its skyline and the wilder hills of Hoy visible in the distance. The monuments are disposed in the landscape on a grandly spacious scale. The two giant circles are on either side of a spit of land, with a gap now closed by a short roadbridge, between two inland lochs called Harray and Stenness. A few hundred metres to the east of this spit is Maes Howe, the greatest chambered mound in northern Britain, and many smaller chambered mounds and standing stones can be found in the hills and fields around. The best general view of the centre is from the hilltop earthworks of the Ring of Bookan (whose stones have all disappeared) in the field across the road from Bookan Farm to the north of Brodgar. As at Stonehenge and Carnac, no habitations have yet been found near the sacred centre itself, but six miles (ten kilometres) to the north-west lies Skara Brae, one of the most famous of all Neolithic villages in Europe (there is an equally well-preserved village in the Shetland islands, even further north).

Recent excavations have shown that the ten houses at Skara Brae, close to the shore of the pretty Bay of Skaill on the west coast of Orkney Mainland, were built and inhabited between 3100 and 2450 BC.

75. Megalithic house built between 3100 and 2450 BC, one of a village of ten houses at Skara Brae on the west coast of Orkney Mainland. From left to right the larger furnishings are a bed (which could be filled with bracken or heather), a hearth in the centre of the house, and a dresser for storage and a work surface.

The designs developed gradually over that period, and the houses were sheltered by a huge midden or pile of waste that the inhabitants threw out over the years. One of the houses was a work place, rather than a habitation. As at Westray, the houses were built of thick stone walls and doubtless had roofs of timber posts and some sort of thatch. The furnishings are much more sophisticated than in the Westray houses – the hearths are formally laid out, there are many cupboards and storage places in the walls and they are equipped with large 'dressers' against the walls, probably used both for work and for keeping household objects. There are human-length enclosures of stone slabs against other walls, which the people apparently filled with bracken or heather to make their beds. They used pestles and mortars and their diet was similar to that of the men and women at Papa Westray, with the addition of more cereals and bottom-feeding sea fish (Clarke 1976, 22). They wore personal ornaments, most commonly beads of seashells, some of which were found scattered – a disastrous storm seems to

have swamped the houses and ended habitation there. The meat they
ate was usually from animals killed at a young age, obviously to provide
tender flesh rather than the maximum amount to eat. It has often been
alleged that the Skara Brae houses were built of stone because of a
shortage of timber in Orkney. But this was done by choice and not
necessity, for it has now been proved that there was a large supply of
driftwood tree-trunks on the Orkney beaches at this time (Clarke 1976,
24–5). Many strange little stones carved with linear decoration were
found in the houses. These may have had practical uses but seem more
likely to be ritual or magical objects. These clues may be read as one
more confirmation that at least some megalithic communities of
farmers maintained a special group of wise men and women, perhaps
rulers as well as sages. Unless other villages of stone houses are found
nearer to Stenness, there must be a strong possibility that the people
who lived at Skara Brae were those who supervised the construction of
the Maes Howe mound and the two big circles six miles (ten kilometres) away at Stenness, and conducted seasonal and eclipse ceremonies there. It may also be that the coincidence of the latest dwelling
date at Papa Westray and of the earliest date at Skara Brae is significant
– the ritual centre of Orkney may have been moved to the sacred site at
Stenness around 3100 BC. If there is anything in this theory, then
another special village inhabited later by these people may await dis-

Fig. 33. Plan of the megalithic village of Skara Brae, beside the Bay of Skaill on the
west coast of Orkney Mainland, six miles north-west of the great stone circles.

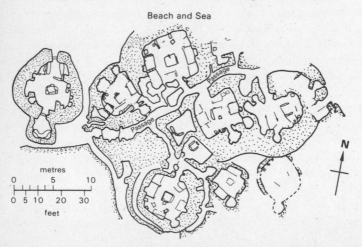

Beach and Sea

covery somewhere; for the second great ring, Brodgar, was probably built after Skara Brae was buried under storm-tossed sand and evacuated around 2400 BC.

The central monuments around Stenness were probably started a century or two after 3000 BC. Maes Howe has been dated to 2800 BC, when the surrounding henge (i.e. ditch and embankment) was dug. The smooth curve of the mound rises only to 24 feet (7.3 metres) in height, but it dominates its surroundings with its majestic presence. Inside the chamber, however, the feeling is much more dramatic. The space is defined by mighty corner buttresses which also support the walls of horizontal stone courses as they close in to form a corbelled roof 13 feet (4 metres) above the floor. A further dimension is added to the space by the three cells which open off from the main chamber at waist height. However great the importance of the neighbouring circles was, it is impossible to escape the feeling that here, and in the wide enclosure around the barrow, lies the heart of the Orkney megaliths. Many other chambered mounds (notably Cuween Hill and Wideford Hill) on Mainland follow its general plan, while others – such as the nearby Unstan mound – have a chamber divided by slabs of stone.

The entrance to Maes Howe faces south-west, towards the Barnhouse Stone, a large standing stone in a field near the Stromness to Kirkwall main road. A few hundred metres north-west of the Barnhouse

76. The chambered mound of Maes Howe, Orkney, in its landscape.

Stone, towards the water of the lochs, there stand the remaining stones of the first great Orkney circle, known as the Stones of Stenness. The actual stones of Stenness are higher than those of any other circle except Stonehenge, and although only three of the big stones are left, the site is vastly impressive in its open setting against the distant hills. Originally there were probably twelve stones of this size and some broken stumps are still visible. The shapes of the stones were clearly intentional, for the slab rising to a point on one side recurs at Brodgar (and at Callanish in the Outer Hebrides). Stenness is a henged monument surrounded by a circular ditch – now almost filled with soil – which was cut deeply into the bedrock. The ditch was not defensive, but had some other purpose or symbolism, for there is a wide level causeway on the northern side. An odd formation of stones can be seen within the circle now, like a rifle foresight aimed at Maes Howe. A square setting of stone slabs was also found in the centre of the circle when it was excavated – it is buried now, but contained gravel mixed

77. Detail of the corbelled stone structure of the chamber of Maes Howe, built about 2800 BC.

78. The remains of the early great stone circle known as the Stones of Stenness, probably built about 2700 BC. The diameter of the ring was only 100 feet (30.7 metres), but the stones were among the tallest in stone circles anywhere.

with charcoal, burned bones and broken pottery (Ritchie and Ritchie 1978, 47). The circle has been dated at 2700 BC and is a prime example of the early type of monumental ring, whose chief use was clearly as a magnificent sacred centre, whatever its subsidiary use as an astronomical observatory in conjunction with the outlying menhirs.

Apart from the Barnhouse Stone to the south-east, another big outlying stone stands almost north-west of the circle. This is the 18-feet (5.5-metres) high Watch Stone, close to the water of the Loch of Stenness. Two other stones previously stood a small distance away; one of

79. The tallest stone of the Stenness ring, with a human figure for scale.

them was called the Stone of Odin and had a hole through it. Promises sealed by clasped hands through this hole were held to be unbreakable, until the stone itself was broken up in 1814.

The road crosses the bridge over the short stretch of water between the two promontories, passes another standing stone in a field on the left and few hundred metres later the broad Ring of Brodgar can be seen ahead. Before reaching it, there is yet another menhir in the heather on the left of the road – the Comet Stone, which is east of the circle's centre – and many mounds and later barrows can be seen gathered around the great ring.

The Ring of Brodgar (sometimes spelt Brogar) covers an area as large as any other megalithic circle except the huge outer ring of stones at Avebury in England – it is exactly the same size as the two inner circles at Avebury. The ring was probably built a century or so before 2000 BC, though it has not been excavated and scientifically dated. Certainly it is clear that sheer display was not so important here as in

80. The Ring of Brodgar, the second of the two great stone circles built in Orkney. It is thought to have been built a little before 2000 BC. The outlying Comet Stone can be seen on the left.

the Stenness ring, for although the Brodgar circle is larger, its individual stones are smaller less than 10 feet (3 metres) high on average.

As with all the major group of Orkney monuments, Brodgar is a henge. Again, the ditch was cut 10 feet (3 metres) down into solid rock, so it must have been important although its two broad causeways make it clear that it is not defensive. It is quite likely that the ditch simply defined the sacred area or perhaps it served some function in the site's use as an observatory. For Alexander Thom has demonstrated very clearly that Brodgar was laid out according to the universal megalithic unit of measurement (2.72 feet), that its original sixty standing stones were arranged in a true circle with a diameter of 125 such megalithic yards (i.e. 340 feet or 103.6 metres) and that there are six degrees of the circle between each stone. The centre is marked and at this point the feeling of the place, with the perfect circle around one and the hills ringing the skyline, is of complete harmony.

Professor Thom has analysed Brodgar carefully and has come to the conclusion that the ring itself played a comparatively small functional part in the astronomical observatory of which it was the focus. He believed that most of the significant lunar alignments and observation points are provided by the mounds and outlying stones surrounding it (Thom 1973 and 1975). From these points, high cliffs on Hoy island and other hills would serve as distant foresights for the rising or setting moon. Strange things happen to the moon's apparent path in the sky at latitudes as far north as Orkney (and at Callanish, as we shall see in the next chapter). At its major standstill (see the introduction for a brief astronomical explanation) the moon here appears to revolve in a great circle around the north polar axis in the sky, during its highest trajectory, so that it scarcely sets – in Shetland and northwards it does not set at all at this phase. During its low trajectory stage in the major standstill, it skims barely above the horizon. These observations would enable a widespread body of knowledge of the moon's movements, assuming that such existed throughout Britain and perhaps on continental Europe, to be refined in a way that more southerly observers could not achieve. As for the ring itself, it may be that its part in the life of the astronomers and the local farmers involved sacred ceremonies rather than astronomy. Equally, it may have further secrets about its use which it has not yet yielded – there is certainly further work to be done there, for Thom's analysis assumed a date later than radiocarbon calibration has now shown to be likely. It is curious that Beaker pottery is so rarely found in Orkney, for those people seem to have played an

81. Part of the Ring of Brodgar. Its diameter of 340 feet (105 metres) is larger than any other circle except Avebury. It is a perfect circle, originally with 60 standing stones placed six degrees apart from each other. Like Maes Howe and Stenness, it is a henged monument, with a surrounding ditch cut deep into solid rock.

important part in the development of megalithic observatories elsewhere in the British Isles. The explanation may be one that carries far-reaching implications for the nature of Neolithic society – that the long-established Orcadian culture co-operated with southern astronomers in pursuing studies of the moon, but excluded the Beaker settlers from their islands, for the most part.

Brodgar probably continued in use as an observatory until the deterioration of the weather in around 1500 BC made the skies cloudy. The area of the Stenness monuments was still regarded as sacred for many centuries, for numerous later cist burials have been found in the fields. Even today it would take a singularly closed mind to leave the Orkney megalithic centre without a feeling that one has visited one of earth's most blessed places.

The megaliths of Scotland have many different types of design, some of them restricted to quite small regions of the country. The most important of these should be mentioned here to give an idea of the wide range.

The culture of which Orkney was probably the centre was not restricted to those islands – all over north-western Scotland there are examples of the distinctive chambered mound or cairn of the Orkney stalled cairn sort. Long barrows of the period before 3000 BC exist in many parts of the British Isles – in Scotland they take a horned shape in plan. Good examples can be found at Coille na Borgie, Skelpick and Camster in the extreme north. But excavation at Camster has shown that the long barrow was built over an earlier round mound, so it does not seem clear whether the Scottish form was contemporary with the major long barrow typical of England and Wales.

In the wide Inverness valley at the northern end of the Great Glen (which divides the Scottish Highlands diagonally into two, from south-west to north-east) there are numerous cairns surrounded by stone circles. These are usually called Clava cairns, after the cluster of those at Balnuaran of Clava seven miles east of Inverness, and they are the only sizeable group of chambered mounds within stone circles in Great Britain. But they are not like their geographically nearest cousins, the round dolmens of Denmark. The standing stones are slabs, unlike the rounded forms of the Danish boulders. Some of the Clava cairns are of the type called passage graves, with capstone roofs; but others simply have a circular mass of drystone walling inside the circle of standing stones, with an uncovered round shaft in the centre of this cairn (see Henshall 1963 and 1972, and Burl 1976, 162). Whether the stone circles had an astronomical purpose or not is as yet undecided. Signs of mysterious rites have been found both inside and outside the cairns (Burl 1976, 165–6) and a few human bones are recorded. Unfortunately, no datable material has yet been recovered.

82. Isle of Lewis, Outer Hebrides. The Trushel Stone at Ballantrushel, a few miles north of Callanish. This is probably the tallest solitary menhir in Scotland. The bottle at its foot gives an idea of the scale.

There are many forms of Scottish megaliths (see Henshall 1963 and 1972, and other guides to Scottish sites), but one in particular must be mentioned here. Aberdeenshire in north-east Scotland has the greatest concentration of circles anywhere and over seventy of them are of the type known as recumbent stone circles. Most of these have twelve stones, and all have one (or occasionally more than one) especially large stone flat on the ground, while the others are standing. The horizontal stone is often of a different rock quarried far away and it is always along the side of the circle facing in the arc between about south and south-west. Cupmarks on stones, white quartz pebbles scattered on the ground, human remains and traces of fires are common to many of these circles. Such finds have led to speculation about human sacrifice, but the evidence does not support that idea. Datable material has shown that they were probably built between 2500 and 1800 BC (Burl 1976, 174, radiocarbon dates calibrated).

Farther south in Scotland, the densest distributions of stone circles are in Perthshire (where a square setting called a Four Poster is also found) and in the south-west around Wigtown. Henged monuments exist in other parts of Scotland as well as in Orkney – the ruined circle at Cairnpapple, south-west of Edinburgh, is the outstanding example. The Isle of Arran, at the mouth of the Clyde, has many megaliths and has been used to demonstrate the theory that each chambered mound (or cairn) may have been the cult centre for a family or community farming a particular stretch of land (Renfrew 1973, 133). The observatories in Argyll at Kintraw, Ballochroy and Temple Wood – famous from the researches carried out there by Alexander Thom – have been described in the section on astronomy in the introduction to this book. But the most famous site of all in Scotland, if we may treat Orkney as something rather separate and special, is the group of great avenues and circles of Callanish.

Callanish owes something of its special quality to its sheer remoteness. It stands on the moors of the west coast of the Isle of Lewis, in the Outer Hebrides. The voyage in the car ferry from Ullapool on the mainland to Stornaway on Lewis is a long one and often stormy. In contrast, the landscape of the island consists of peaceful moorland, with the peat-gatherers' trenches dug deep, and rocky but rounded hills. The coasts of Lewis have a fair number of megalithic monuments, but few chambered cairns. It seems that it was the relatively late Beaker culture which gave the area its importance. At Ballantrushel, some kilometres north along the coast from Callanish, there stands the 20-feet (6-metres) high Trushel Stone, a solitary menhir of the type which may have been used as a local foresight for astronomical observation and apparently the highest of its kind in Scotland. An oval house (dated to 2100 BC) of the Beaker people has been found at Northton, not too far from Callanish, and the district is redolent of their preoccupation with the study of the skies. It is likely that traces of other Beaker settlements

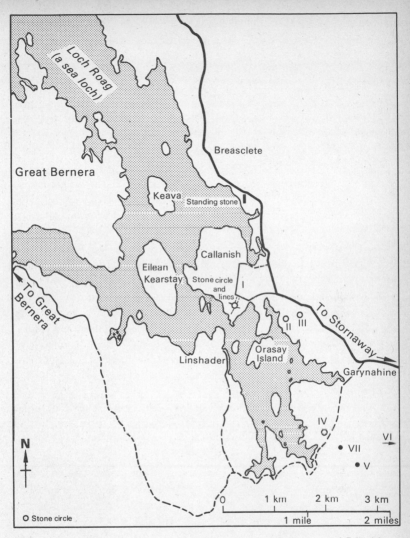

Fig. 34. Outline map of the area around the stone circles and alignments of Callanish, on the west coast of the Isle of Lewis, Outer Hebrides, Scotland.

lie hidden under the peat which started to blanket the farming soil when the fine sub-boreal weather ended around 1500 BC.

No other megalithic site exceeds the lyrical beauty of Callanish's setting above Loch Roag, which is a sea loch. After crossing the centre of the island from Stornaway, the stones of the avenue and main

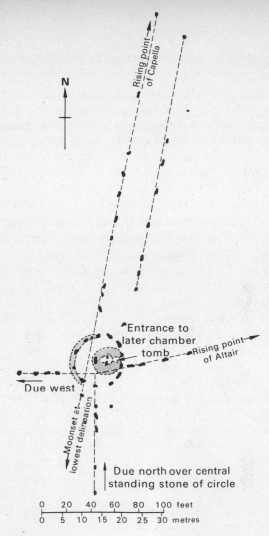

N

Rising point of Capella

Entrance to
later chamber
tomb

Rising point
of Altair

Due west

Moonset at
lowest delineation

Due north over central
standing stone of circle

| 0 | 20 | 40 | 60 | 80 | 100 feet |
| 0 | 5 | 10 | 15 | 20 | 25 | 30 metres |

Fig. 35. Plan of the alignments and main circle at Callanish, with some of the
significant astronomical lines.

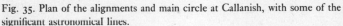

83. Callanish, Isle of Lewis. The circle and alignments on the ridge projecting into the
sea loch, Loch Roag.

circle are seen outlined on their ridge against the sky. A stone circle and then another can be seen among the heather from the road as the great site is approached. The small and scattered crofts of Callanish village end quite close to the stones, but there is no hotel and the place is unspoilt.

The position of the monument is a remarkable example of the siting of megaliths in the landscape (this apparent system is described in the introduction and has been noted at sites in many other parts of Europe mentioned in this book). The Callanish stones are on a ridge which drops away to a wide bowl in the hills; the horizon is largely surrounded by protective ridges while to the north-west the loch opens out towards the sea.

The main Callanish circle is properly approached between the two rows of standing stones forming an avenue 270 feet (82.5 metres) long from the north. Three other much shorter single alignments of standing stones run out from the circle due west, due south and just north of east. Among the pairs of stones facing each other across the double avenue, there are examples of that coupling of rounded shapes with tall thin forms seen in other avenues such as Avebury. The circle itself is of tall granite stones of haunting shapes and twisted stratification. The tallest stone is over 15 feet (4.6 metres) high and stands almost in the centre of the ring, which is of the 'flattened circle' plan often found. This central stone, but none of the others, is of the slab type – with one corner higher than the other – also seen in the Orkney circles. Beside the Callanish central stone, a small chamber tomb was later inserted within the ring – its entrance faces due east. South of the circle and lines, there is an outcrop of rock at the point where the ridge drops towards the lochside – this has apparently been ignored in the past, but it is imposing enough to have been of cult significance in itself, as with outcrops in similar positions in Belgium and Corsica which we have described.

Callanish has been investigated and analysed by many people (notably by Somerville 1913, Hawkins 1966, Thom 1967, Henshall 1972 and by two local teachers, Ponting and Ponting 1977). It has certainly been clearly demonstrated that it could be used as a lunar (and solar) observatory, and the moon's behaviour at major and minor standstills is almost as remarkable here as it is a little farther north in Orkney. But the main circle at Callanish should not be thought of in isolation. We have mentioned the two smaller circles to the east of it, which are in easy sight of the main ring – one of them is a fair-sized ellipse quite

84. A pair of stones facing each other across the northern avenue of Callanish.

close to the water's edge, while the other is an elliptical ring within a circle. In addition, there is another stone circle less than two miles away in a south-south-east direction (precisely hidden from sight of the big circle by a hillock), quite close to the road that runs around the end of Loch Roag. On the hill to the south-east of this circle, on the other side of the road, one upright stone remains of another small megalithic group – this site, Airidh nam Bideram, seems to have been an important observation point visible from the main Callanish circle. Professor

85. The main circle of Callanish, probably built a century or two before 2000 BC.

Thom has numbered these monuments as Callanish I (the main circle) to Callanish V in the order we have just mentioned them; he has also noted two other sites, one still further east and the other between IV and V, which he has numbered VI and VII respectively (Thom 1967, 125). The Callanish observatory may have been even more extensive than that, for on the steep hillside above the road bridge across to Great Bernera island there are two more standing stones which are orientated roughly towards peaks on the horizon.

To understand the way in which the extensive observatory at Callanish worked, it is necessary to bear in mind the crucial points in the moon's patterns of movement which are outlined in the introduction. These patterns would be important to the megalith builders for predictions of the tides, of the moon's risings and settings to know the best times for sowing or planting (a belief which still persists in folklore) and for ritual purposes, and of eclipses, when the orderly progress of the sun or moon was interrupted. At the chief circle of Callanish, the stones were arranged in such a way that they indicated various key rising and setting places on the horizon, in conjunction with particular hilltops on the skyline. The central line of the long avenue meets the extended lines of the east and west alignments at a point near, but not

86. The highest stone, over 15 feet (4.75 metres) tall, near the centre of the main Callanish circle. The small chamber tomb at its foot is believed to have been added later.

on, the centre of the circle – from that same point, a line drawn through another standing stone (and along the axis of an oval of low stones just outside the circle) indicates the midsummer sunrise precisely. The two lines of the main avenue may have been used in both directions. Looking south along either (i.e. towards the circle), the moon at its lowest declination would be seen to set over a mountain called Clisham sixteen miles away on the horizon. Looking north, the lines of stones would have pointed to the rising place of the first-magnitude star Capella in 1800 BC. At that time, the single line of stones pointing just north of east from the circle would have indicated the rising place of another first-magnitude star, Altair. The easterly alignment, of course, points to the sunrise at the equinox, while the line running north–south could be used from the natural outcrop of rock to give a bearing on the polar axis when studying the wheeling of the stars. This north–south line ends at the tallest stone, near the centre of the ring, which is orientated in that direction.

It was impossible to find distinguishable horizon markers for all important risings and settings from the main site, and Thom believes that the smaller outlying circles were erected at suitable places to observe these other events. For example, the line from the circle he has numbered II to the two standing stones numbered VI was an important lunar declination. From site V, Airidh nam Bideram, the moon would rise at its farthest south over noticeable mountains on the horizon to the south-south-east – from the same site, the moon would set at its farthest north above the circle numbered II (Thom 1967, 127 and 1971, 69). The principle that Callanish was a widespread observatory is now widely accepted, but Thom himself has pointed out that further analysis and archaeological examination are needed before the individual observation lines can be established. Apart from anything else, it now seems that Callanish was probably built before 2000 BC, so the positions of the celestial bodies at that time should be recalculated. If archaeological research confirms that the monument was built by the Beaker people, we may well guess that it was their extreme northern observatory, intended to investigate the moon's behaviour at that latitude with data which they could not get from the Orkney people. The nearest avenues similar to those of Callanish are in Cumbria in England.

There remains the question of Callanish's use for other purposes. There is no reason why the scientific functions of the main group should not have been fulfilled by stones the height of a man – indeed it

87. The Bernera stones, on a steep hillside above the road bridge across to Great Bernera island, a few kilometres from Callanish. The big slabs are aligned roughly towards peaks on the horizon.

is the lines of stones that seem to be pointers, rather than the stones in the circle itself. The symbolism of the ring as the centre of all activities there seems obvious and its sacred nature is hard to doubt. The ancient Greek historian Diodorus mentioned a temple in the extreme west where the moon god danced every eighteen years (the lunar cycle), and this has been taken to mean Callanish or perhaps Stonehenge. As a temple, Callanish's deities were surely celestial bodies, although it has been argued that water was also a sacred element there (Burl 1976, 153–4). Hardly a scrap of archaeological evidence has been found on the site, but there is a persistent local legend that the stones were erected by the slaves of a great priest-king dressed in robes of mallard feathers, who came to Callanish with many ships. Waterfowl and clothes made from their feathers were widely associated with centres of healing during the first millennium BC, especially if linked with sun worship (Ross 1967, 279). We do not know whether that legend or the association with healing go back as far as the people who built

Callanish. But if they do, we may imagine the special significance of this remote sanctuary and the sort of processions and rites that would take place along the ridge and among the high stones.

The open sea of the Atlantic coast near Callanish is subject to more violent storms today than almost any other part of the British Isles. The lovely area around the megalithic site itself is usually clouded and damp, though the hills shelter it from the worst of the gales. It feels a special place, without doubt, but a cold one. In 2000 BC the climate was very different. The soil was good for farming, the summers were warm, and even in winter the visibility was usually clear for sightings far across the hills to the rising moon or sun beyond.

Neolithic farmers may have settled in Ireland earlier than anywhere else in the British Isles. Houses and pits found at Ballynagilly in County Tyrone have yielded a date of around 4700 BC, with a possible error of about a century either way (MacKie 1977, 165, date calibrated). This is about the same as the date of the earliest megalithic structure at Carnac, but in Ireland the first date for a monument is about 3700 BC, for the earthwork enclosure of Knockiveagh. There are many large chambered mounds in the north of the country, and Newgrange, Ireland's greatest monument, dates from a few centuries after Knockiveagh. Newgrange will be described later in this chapter.

Near Limerick in south-west Ireland, the area around Lough Gur is rich in megaliths dating from 3500 BC onwards – there are several small chambered mounds and stone circles, as well as one of the most impressive henge circles anywhere. This is the Lios, a unique monument in several ways. The whole structure is surrounded by a massive circular earthwork. The circle of standing stones supports the inner side of the earthwork, leaving a large round area open inside. There is only one rather narrow entrance to this enclosed circle, which has a diameter of 155 feet (47 metres) inside the embankment. Some of the standing stones are very large, one of them remarkably so, but the interior was empty and flattened when it was in use – the builders carefully paved it with clay which must have given a good smooth surface when the weather was fine.

The evidence indicates that the Lios was built between 3000 and 2500 BC, after which the Beaker people moved into the area, but its purpose is still unknown. A large amount of broken pottery was excavated there, apparently smashed on purpose as megalith-building people seem to have done in many places. This is perhaps suggestive of big gatherings of people in the circle, of festivals with dancing and drinking – these celebrations may have had a ritual significance, but one can

88. Ireland. Menhir near the Punchtown Racecourse at Naas, near Dublin. This stone, which is 17 feet (5.3 metres) high, is part of an extensive group of menhirs, circles and dolmens in this district.

hardly resist the thought that perhaps they were just jolly parties. Certainly 200 or 300 people could fit into the enclosure without undue crowding. Other suggestions are that the Lios was a market, a moot or an astronomical observatory – significant lunar lines have indeed been detected there, and there are other circles in the surrounding fields which could form a complex of observation points. The henge was in effect part of a farm when visited in 1977, in good condition and surrounded by high trees and deep grass; the Irish government unfortunately plans to develop it as a tourist site and no doubt its rustic atmosphere will have gone soon.

The other great stone ring of Ireland is near the north-east coast. This is Ballynoe circle, in the soft land east of the Mountains of Mourne in County Down. Within its large outer ring, most of an inner circle survives around a small mound containing several stone cists. There is also another inner setting of stones like a crescent. Ballynoe is thought to be an early monument, probably of 3000 BC or so.

The people of the Beaker culture moved very swiftly into much of Ireland after 2500 BC, bringing the first use of metal. They did not penetrate all areas, however. In the extreme south-west of the country – beyond Cork – another people were building at least eighty stone circles between 2500 and 2000 BC. These bear a remarkable resemblance to the 'recumbent stone' circles which we have mentioned in Aberdeenshire. The question of whether this was coincidence or whether these people were linked to those 500 miles away in Scotland, has caused much controversy. The Irish rings have the characteristic large stone lying in the same quarter of the circle. Many other features are the same, too, but there are equally noticeable differences. A computer analysis in 1973 showed that twenty-seven out of thirty circles examined had detectable alignments relating to the sun, the moon, the planet Venus or major stars (Burl 1976, 222, quoting Barber 1973). One of the best examples, Drombeg in County Cork, has been excavated and provided evidence of complicated rituals. Many of these circles, and others in Ireland, have carefully laid paving or levelled gravel within or outside the rings. The way in which these surfaces are arranged has been taken to indicate dancing or processions.

Among other Irish monuments, we must mention the henges, circles, dolmens and very tall menhirs around Naas, south of Dublin; the magnificence of the monuments around Sligo; the alignments, each of three standing stones, around Belfast; and the complexes of many circles and lines of small stones near Beaghmore, south-west of

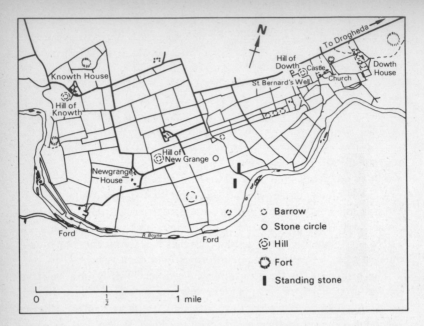

Fig. 36. Outline map of the Bend in the Boyne, west of Drogheda, Ireland, showing the three large chambered mounds – Knowth, Newgrange and Dowth.

Londonderry in County Tyrone – which date from the centuries around 2000 B C.

The most famous megalithic monument in Ireland, however, was built long before that. A few kilometres east of Drogheda in County Meath, the river Boyne makes a large curve to the south. This is the well-known Bend in the Boyne and inside its loop are three enormous man-made hillocks. To the west, the Hill of Knowth is at present being excavated and restored (it has two chambers and many satellite barrows). To the east, the Hill of Dowth has been very little altered by archaeologists as yet – two small passages and chambers are known in one side of it, while some of the kerbstones (including one finely carved) around its foot have been revealed. Between these two, and a little to the south, lies one of the finest megalithic monuments of all, Newgrange.

Perhaps only Avebury, Stonehenge and the alignments of Carnac can take the breath away as Newgrange does. For visual splendour no other chambered mound in Europe can compared with it.

89. The Bend in the Boyne, west of Drogheda, Ireland. The Hill of Dowth, one of the group of three huge man-made mounds. The other two hills, Knowth and Newgrange, were in this sort of state before excavation.

90. The Bend in the Boyne. A ruined stone circle in the foreground and, on the skyline, the hill of Newgrange.

91. Newgrange, with its frontage of white quartz and its surrounding kerb and circle of standing stones. Built about 3400 BC.

A small early mound of the passage-grave type near Knowth is at least two centuries older than any of the three big mounds and it is evident from the many smaller monuments around the valley – barrows, standing stones and the remains of a small circle – this was a sacred area over a very long period. None of the Boyne mounds is positioned in the cradled type of megalithic site often found at other places visited – the feeling here is of the builders seeking a high place for each of the three huge barrows, dominating the valley.

Newgrange (it is often spelt New Grange) has had its southern side restored to the form in which it was built. The date of its construction is at the latest 3000 BC and, if radiocarbon dates are calibrated with Suess's graph, it was 3400 BC. The frontage is of gleaming white quartz, studded with other stones, which makes the whole hill shine from the distance. As one approaches, the shape and the architectural detail seem quite unbelievably sophisticated for a Neolithic farming community, and one cannot help sympathizing with those who look to flying saucers for the origin of the megaliths – in fact, if the hill of Newgrange floated away from its site it could be very similar to the flying objects so often reported. But the builders of the mound were not just primitive farmers. They were as intelligent and imaginative as any modern men and women – we have seen evidence of their remarkable religious beliefs, science and building achievements elsewhere. Given the prosperity and the labour to erect this temple to the sun and its rebirth, there is no reason to be surprised by their ability to design with such powerful originality.

For whatever else Newgrange is, it is primarily a temple. Collective burial was normally performed in the great chambered monuments of north-west Europe around 3000 BC – the long German and Dutch enclosures incorporated cells for this purpose, as did the long barrows of Great Britain and the sacred mounds of Brittany – but we are confident that their primary purpose was seasonal gatherings to invoke the deities of nature. At Newgrange the focus was certainly on the rebirth of the sun at the winter solstice. The concave middle of the frontage, around the entrance, probably formed the centre of the ritual ceremonies. It seems likely that large numbers of people would attend these, perhaps gathered in the broad meadow beyond the outlying circle of standing stones (some of which survive) around the monument. At the winter solstice the sages conducting the ceremony might well start the proceedings in this concave bay outside the hill. But at dawn they would perhaps move along the 62-feet (19-metres) passage into the big corbelled

92. The entrance to Newgrange, with the famous decorated slab and the slit above the doorway which allows the sun to penetrate to the chamber at the midwinter sunrise.

chamber, to witness the great moment. This came when the rising sun shone through the horizontal slit above the entrance and illuminated the spiral carvings on the walls of the stone room, with its three subsidiary cells, far inside. This phenomenon still happens at Newgrange at the winter solstice, and for only a day or two on either side of it. When it ceases, the winter sun has safely started its progression towards the summer once again and another year is secure.

The purpose of the circle of standing stones around Newgrange is not known. Nor is it certain that it was built at the same time as the

93. The corbelled roof structure of the chamber within Newgrange.

94. Carvings on the roof of one of the side cells in the chamber of Newgrange.

barrow. But it reflects another circle of low slabs, the kerb which runs all around the foot of the quartz-covered wall. Most of those stone slabs are undecorated, but the stone in front of the entrance and that at the opposite side of the mound are covered with the same sort of spirals and other patterns as are found on several rocks inside the chamber These patterns are similar to those in megalithic monuments elsewhere – for example, in the other great chambered mound of Gavr'inis near Carnac, in several temples in Malta (which are of much the same date as Newgrange), in tombs in Sicily and on numerous stones from Scotland to Spain in the form called cup-and-ring marks. The chief motifs are the spiral and the concentric circle, and we speculate about their significance in the introduction of this book.

The deterioration of Newgrange, which left it a hump covered with grass and trees in recent times, may well have started with the arrival of the Beaker people soon after 2500 BC. Their dislike of collective burial has been demonstrated elsewhere by the closing of the Neolithic chambered monuments. By the year 2000 BC they had settled in large tracts of the Irish countryside. Occasionally, the remains of their wooden and clay-daubed houses are found (several have been detected around Cork). But in Ireland their main traces are the small stone circles. These were one aspect of the earlier people's work which the Beaker people seem to have taken up with enthusiasm. We have already mentioned the hundreds of Bronze Age stone circles found in many parts of Ireland – it seems that all those rings may be descended from the big circle around Newgrange and the other monumental circles described earlier. We cannot yet be sure whether the study of the skies, which went with the late rings, was also the legacy of the Neolithic builders of the Lios, Ballynoe and Newgrange – a thorough analysis of the astronomical possibilities of those sites may show how much science was pursued there.

15   England and Wales – Avebury

Despite the impressive megalithic groups in many other countries described in this book, Carnac in France together with Avebury and Stonehenge in England are justly known as the greatest achievements of that age in western Europe. At its full flowering just before and just after the introduction of metal working to the north-western parts of the continent, those places may be seen as the centres of a loosely linked megalith-building culture with wide outposts where the peoples developed their own variations of the general architectural types. As we began this survey of European monuments with Brittany, we shall end it with Wales and England, and in particular the area known as Wessex which is the ancient heart of England (see map on page 189).

Mesolithic settlements of people who gathered wild crops and hunted animals have been found around the coasts of England and Wales, but recent evidence seems to show that there were farmers in some parts two or three centuries before 4000 BC (MacKie 1977, 165 ff). Early calibrated radiocarbon dates include one from a flint mine of about 4300 BC and another from Hembury causewayed camp in Devon of 4200 BC. The earliest chambered mounds with collective burials date from a little after 4000 BC and during the next few centuries the famous long barrows started to appear. These typically have a complex stone chamber, often with a frontage of standing stones, at one end of a long earthwork platform.

It may be that the long barrow type of monument was first developed in Wales or western England. A line of them can be traced along the south Wales coast – Parc Cwm (west of Swansea), Tinkinswood and St Lythans (west of Cardiff) and Portskewett (south-west of the Severn roadbridge) are good examples. Further south-west, there are many in Gloucestershire, Somerset and in Wessex – the area stretching from Dorset through Wiltshire to the Thames valley. One of the finest is Wayland's Smithy on the Ridgeway track east of Swindon – its

95. England. Two of the three aligned menhirs called the Devil's Arrows, on the outskirts of Boroughbridge, Yorkshire. The tallest of the three is 18 feet (5.6 metres) high and the stones seem to be carved – despite theories that they have weathered into this shape.

earliest part was built about 3600 BC, while its present form dates from 2800 BC. They are spread widely around the English coastline; Hunters Burgh (north-west of Eastbourne in Sussex) and Spellow Hills (north-west of Skegness in Lincolnshire) are typical of the positions a few kilometres inland. And they spread further too. The type of long barrow with a plan like horns is found in south-west and northern Scotland, while the raised enclosures which we have mentioned in Denmark, Germany and the Netherlands have evident similarities. Some archaeologists have also suggested links with monuments found in France and Poland. We shall describe one of the Wessex examples in some detail later, but it must be mentioned here that these long barrows were certainly the 'temples' as well as the burial-places of the early Neolithic people. As burial-places they were apparently restricted to members of a special group of people in the farming communities.

Other sorts of chambered mounds or dolmens of the Neolithic period are found in various parts of England. Round barrows were apparently favoured in Yorkshire. The dolmens in Kent seem to have been built by a largely isolated people – Kit's Coty, north of Maidstone, may date from around 3000 BC. Other impressive dolmens are found in Cornwall, especially on the Land's End peninsula, and in much of Wales. Bryn Celli Dhu on Anglesey is a dolmen-type mound built in an earlier henged earthwork circle. Flint mines were started in several parts of England fairly early, and a wide trade in flints certainly brought various communities into contact with each other. Grimes Graves, near Thetford in Norfolk, is the most extensive of their flint mines, but others have been found in several parts of England.

The other early large-scale works of these people were the Causewayed Camps. Traces of these exist in many areas of southern England, sometimes overbuilt with later earthworks of the following 3000 years. If the date already mentioned for Hembury in Devon is correct, some of the causewayed camps were started before 4000 BC. But most of them were probably built during the centuries leading up to 3000 BC. In Wessex, these big camps included Maiden Castle near Dorchester (subsequently much enlarged), Hambledon Hill near Sturminster, Whitesheet Hill near Wincanton, Robin Hood's Hall fairly near Stonehenge, Knap Hill above the Vale of Pewsey and Windmill Hill (which we shall describe later on, with Avebury). The camps consisted of rings of earth banks and ditches, with a central enclosed area. Broad causeways of level earth run from the perimeter to the central enclosure.

The use of the causewayed camps has caused much controversy.

Large quantities of waste from food, especially animal bones, were dumped in their ditches. It may be that the farmers of the area wintered here and sheltered their cattle behind the embankments. Some people may have lived in the camps the whole year. It is quite likely, however, that they were the gathering places for the people all around at the times of the seasonal festivals suggested in the introduction. The archaeologist Colin Renfrew has suggested that each camp formed the centre of an 'embryonic chiefdom', of which there were several in Wessex (Renfrew 1976, 229). It is quite evident that these were peaceful times, for there is no sign of defences at the camps and the causeways are very different from the complex fortified entrances of later earthworks.

By 3000 BC, the Wessex people were developing the idea of the causewayed camps' earthworks into other ditched and embanked monuments called henges. These were probably for ritual purposes and inside the roughly circular earthworks they normally built structures of some kind. For the origins of these we must look to the west again. As early as 3700 BC a round ditched enclosure at Knockiveagh in Ireland contained pits of debris which seem to indicate rites linking holes in the ground with fertility (Burl 1976, 21). The henges developed on both sides of the Irish Sea – Llandegai near Caernarvon dated from about 3500 BC – and then spread all over Britain. An earthwork henge of about 3400 BC can even be seen at Arminghall outside Norwich, in an area where there are no megaliths.

The structures within the henged enclosure were often built of timber. At Arminghall there was a big horseshoe-shaped setting of eight immense oak tree-trunks set upright in the ground. Much later, at Woodhenge in Wessex, the famous multiple rings of tree-trunks date from 2300 BC, while the wooden rings at other Wessex sites such as Mount Pleasant and Durrington Walls South are of about 2500 BC.

The henge monuments which remain, however, are of rock – the early stone circles. They are usually difficult to date unless organic materials are found under their foundations. The earliest of all may be the standing stones around the hill of Newgrange in Ireland (a few other examples exist further north), but after that there is no evidence of anything earlier than the first circles in Cumbria which may date from a century or two after 3000 BC. It was not until the years just before 2500 BC that other people in Britain started to build stone circles. But when they started they built on the grandest scale, rather than starting with small structures.

96. England. The Devil's Den dolmen in a valley on the far side of the Ridgeway from Avebury.

These giant early rings are usually referred to as Great Stone Circles. The main groups of them are on Bodmin Moor in Cornwall, Lough Gur in Ireland, North Uist in the Outer Hebrides (where there are four little-known examples in oval formations), Orkney, Dumfriesshire, Cumbria (where there are twelve), the Peak District in Derbyshire, northern Somerset and the part of Wiltshire around Avebury and Stonehenge – other isolated great stone circles can be found in several places. In many particularly large cases the great circles were built within a henged earthwork – these are at Orkney (two) and Cairnpapple in Scotland, The Lios in Ireland, Long Meg and her Daughters in Cumbria, Arbor Low and the Bull Ring in Derbyshire, the Devil's Quoits west of Oxford, Avebury and Stonehenge in Wiltshire and the Stripple Stones in Cornwall. The big stones have disappeared from some of these – Cairnpapple, the Bull Ring and the Devil's Quoits – but the henges remain.

That list of henged great circles omits a small number of the largest monuments – notably Stanton Drew in Somerset, Castle Rigg in Cumbria and the smaller Rollright Stones in Oxfordshire – but the scattered distribution of the henge-rings along the whole length of Great Britain may indicate that each was a regional centre for religious or secular purposes, or both. The building of most great stone circles just precedes the arrival of the first groups of Beaker people in England from 2500 BC onwards. It has therefore sometimes been argued that it was the Beaker people who directed their construction, bringing new ideas and structural techniques with them. That theory does not bear close examination, for there is no evidence of earlier circles in any of the countries from which these people may have emerged (indeed there are comparatively few stone circles outside Britain, as we have seen earlier in this book). In Britain, on the other hand, the stone circles were an extraordinary but curiously logical development from a historical sequence of long barrow (perhaps round barrow in places) – wooden dwelling – causewayed camp – henge earthwork – wood circle – stone circle, over a period of a 1000 years or more. The circular form was surely important to express a religious concept. To clinch the matter, the structures dated 2400 BC at Durrington Walls henge, north of Stonehenge, had only pre-Beaker pottery, while Woodhenge (built in 2300 BC) had Beaker together with pre-Beaker pots.

It seems likely that the Beaker people arrived during a great flowering of religious architecture among the Neolithic people. The great circles were as new then as Victorian cathedrals and churches are today.

There was already a special group of sages or ruler-priests in each community, judging by comparisons which have been made between the food of those who lived close to the henges with that of the ordinary people in the surrounding country (MacKie 1977, 179). At Durrington Walls the presence of the earliest spindle-whorl found in England indicates that by around 2400 BC they had woven fabrics as well as the leather and matted fibres which had probably provided clothing before.

The Neolithic people were building other ambitious monuments and earthworks, as well as the stone circles. Menhirs of great height and varied shapes are found alone or in alignments (such as the tremendous Devil's Arrows at Boroughbridge in Yorkshire) in some parts of the country, while smaller standing stones exist in thousands in hedgerows and in fields wherever farmers have not knocked them down. Many of these have had magic powers ascribed to them – one such is the London Stone now behind railings in the wall of the Bank of China building at 111 Cannon Street, fairly close to the Mansion House in the City of London. Until early in this century it stood alone – in medieval times important announcements were made from beside it and there is a legend that the safety of the city depends on it.

The late Neolithic earthworks are even more imposing than the standing stones. In London few traces remain of the mounds which are said to have stood until recent centuries outside the Tower of London (the White Mound), Westminster Abbey (the Tothill) and on top of Parliament Hill, Hampstead – although there is still a ditched barrow on Hampstead Heath. There is a story that the two hills on either side of the Walbrook stream were also sacred, one of them the site of St Paul's Cathedral today – but such tales are difficult to document. What is sure is that much of south-western England has huge earthworks, many of which go back to late Neolithic times. These people built great mounds – of which Silbury Hill at Avebury is the most famous – and vast enclosures of the type called a Cursus, cut into the chalk and running for considerable distances over the Wessex downs. The Cursus at Stonehenge is well known and can be made out with a little difficulty, but the longest is the Dorset Cursus which runs for six miles across country.

Where they did not build completely man-made hills, the megalith builders often carved existing hills into a particular shape. The best instance of this is the Tor at Glastonbury in Somerset, which may be a natural outcrop in the flat country, but has quite clearly been sculpted

97. Avebury and the surrounding chalk Downs, viewed from the round barrow on top of Windmill Hill, where the great Neolithic causewayed camp of 3200 to 2000 BC is now invisible. Silbury Hill is in the middle of the picture, with the horizontal line of the West Kennet long barrow to the left of its peak. The Avebury circles lie among the trees on the left.

to the shape of a half-pear. The chapel on the Tor is dedicated to St Michael, the dragon saint. Another similarly shaped hill at Abbotsbury in Dorset has a chapel on its peak, as at Glastonbury, dedicated to St Catherine – another dragon saint. The Wrekin in Staffordshire (as far as one can see under its wooded sides) seems to bear the marks of sculpting too, while St Michael's Mount in Cornwall has the half-pear shape – whether by nature or by man's labour. Many others can be seen and they do not seem to be restricted to England. Mont St Michel and its neighbour at Dol can both be recognized as the same type of shape. It should be emphasized that no way is known of dating such land sculpture, which is on a large scale but no larger than the very different English work of the Dark Ages (such as the Wansdyke) or the landscaping which is seen in great areas of China. Some of the earthwork monuments doubtless had astronomical functions (the Dorset Cursus has been analysed fairly convincingly from this point of view – see Wood 1978), and it seems that the sages of the end of the Neolithic period were developing a study of the sun, moon and stars which was integrated into their religious beliefs and practices.

It may well have been in this mathematical and scientific field that the colonizing Beaker people established their eminence after 2400 BC, developing religious astronomy at the hundreds of smaller stone circles built all over western and northern Britain in the next few centuries. They changed at least some of the religious customs. The old long barrows were closed up, perhaps marking a change of location for some seasonal ceremonies as well as the end of the line of men and women who had been buried there. The Beaker people themselves buried their dead singly in low round barrows of several shapes. They developed the mining and use of metal, producing tools and fine objects of bronze or gold. And they brought an elegant new type of pottery decoration, as well as the typical shape of pot from which they have been given their name (see page 21).

The origin of the Beaker people remains controversial among archaeologists who have traced and tried to date the products of their culture in many parts of Europe. One theory is that the settlers came from the Danube basin in central Europe, where metal-working was developed by 4000 BC – this envisages a population explosion or pressure by invaders from Asia which may have caused a wave of people to move west in about 2500 BC and again 300 years later. Another theory sees these people as combining the cultural achievements of the people in southern and central Germany with those of the folk who made

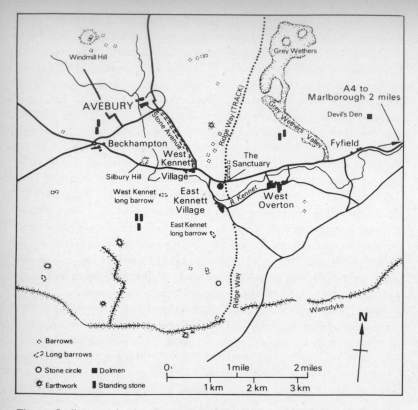

Fig. 37. Outline map showing the megaliths and earthworks around Avebury, England, with the ancient Ridgeway road running north–south near it.

tunnel beakers in the north. A third idea is that the Beaker culture originated in the Iberian peninsula, where other people developed metallurgy before 3000 BC. Examination of their skeletons and skulls reveals a shortish stocky people, with protruding eyebrows, but that has not helped to trace where they came from. What we do know is that they built Woodhenge in about 2300 BC and – perhaps by then completely merged with the earlier Neolithic community in Wessex – they rebuilt Stonehenge 200 years later. There, in strange contrast to their general dislike of really big megaliths, they put up the sarsen-capped outer circle and the horseshoe of giant trilithons which remain its special visual wonders. But then they often seem to have adopted some of the customs and interests of the local people with whom they settled, and a few of the stone settings within the great Neolithic circles of Avebury may also be the result of their pursuit of astronomy.

Avebury – because of the widespread sources of its types of monument – has been called the metropolitan temple of England. Many of its structures are otherwise unknown in Wessex. In a valley three miles to the east of the circles – up a track off the main A4 road – there is a dolmen called the Devil's Den, of a type scarcely found between here and Cornwall. Moreover, although the henge is a common enough monument in Wessex, avenues of standing stones are more typical of Cumbria or Cornwall, while central pillars in circles are a feature of the rings in Shropshire.

The group of monuments at Avebury should be seen in the context of the Ridgeway, the ancient road which winds across England and, with its extensions at either end, provided a route largely on high land between Dorset and the flint mines of Norfolk. The Ridgeway's surviving track runs almost north–south on the hilltop above Avebury, about a mile east of the circles which form the centre of the widely spread sanctuary. Five other stone circles used to exist within a nine-mile radius around Avebury – at Clatford, Langdean Bottom, Coate, Winterbourne Bassett and at Falkners on the slope below the Ridgeway – but few traces of these remain today.

The ideal place to start a visit to Avebury is at the site of the causewayed camp called Windmill Hill. The approach can be seen on the map – when the track becomes too rough for cars, a few minutes' walk brings one to a broad hilltop meadow on which the only feature seems to be a cluster of small round barrows. From the highest barrow there is a broad view over Avebury to the man-made Silbury Hill, with the Ridgeway running along the hills to the left and the chalk Downs rolling smoothly around the horizon. On the surface of the field surrounding this small barrow there are very shallow depressions. When these were excavated, they were found to be the remains, flattened by centuries of ploughing, of a great causewayed camp which had three concentric and roughly circular banks and ditches. The earliest settlement date was about 3700 B C and the camp itself was built around 3250 B C. Most of the animals traced were cattle, but the people kept sheep, goats and pigs as well. They grew a type of wheat called emmer, and barley. They cultivated flax – although they did not weave, they probably matted some sort of material – and evidently made stitched clothes out of leather. They made fine tools of flint and antler. They kept dogs rather like fox terriers, and gathered crab-apples and nuts. The weather

98. The West Kennet long barrow, near Avebury, built in about 3250 BC. Its size, east–west alignment and many other features are similar to the raised enclosures of Denmark, Germany and the Netherlands.

99. The megalithic frontage at the east end of the West Kennet long barrow, which acts as a screen for the multiple burial-chamber within.

was drier than nowadays, with warm clear summers and crisp winters. The causewayed camp was used until at least 2000 BC, well after the arrival of the Beaker people. No dwellings have been found, and it was possibly a gathering place for the people of the region at the time of the seasonal festivals, perhaps for celebrations and probably for markets too.

Their early religious centre and the burial-place of some special sort of people was the West Kennet long barrow, on the other side of Avebury village, two and a half miles south-south-east of the causewayed camp. It is a brisk walk from the main A4 road, on the brow of a hill. West Kennet is one of the grandest of the long barrows whose wide distribution has been described in this chapter. It was built in about 3250 BC, and was used as a collective burial-place until the Beaker people closed it up in 2000 BC. The plan of the great monument is a mound 330 feet (102 metres) long, pointing east–west and narrowing towards the west, with a frontage of megalithic stones at the east end guarding a passage which has five quite large chambers opening off it. The side cells contained the remains of forty-six human-beings, including twelve children, when excavated, but the other spaces had been plundered by a Marlborough doctor in 1685 who made a medicine from the bones. There were originally straight ditches running parallel with the sides of the long mound, but these have disappeared under the surrounding field. The barrow bears obvious resemblances to the long raised enclosures we have described in Denmark and Germany, particularly in its dimensions (it is almost exactly the same length as the Grønjaegers Høj), its orientation and in the great stone frontage at the east end. Doubtless this provided a forecourt for rites other than funerals. The top of the barrow was quite possibly used as a platform for other ceremonies, if the form of the continental monuments is any indication.

From the long barrow, Windmill Hill can be seen in the distance – but between the two there is the largest known man-made mound of the period, Silbury Hill, on the other side of the main road. The hill can usually be climbed and to do so gives a much better impression of its 130-feet (39.6-metres) height than does a distant view. It is one of the most ambitious undertakings of Neolithic building, a gigantic cone with a flattened top and a circular plan. Its interior is formed by great sloping steps of chalk blocks. It was started a little before 2600 BC and built in four stages, occupying a huge labour force and employing previously untried building methods which have easily withstood 4500 years of weathering. Despite several excavations, no burial chamber has been found in it and its purpose must be otherwise explained. There is nothing else like it. One interpretation is that of Michael Dames, who has done a great deal of comparative research and suggests that the mound and surrounding moat are one of many large-scale sculptural representations of the Great Goddess herself (Dames 1976 and 1977). Anyone who has walked along this end of the Ridgeway, or indeed in this part of Wiltshire, will know the impact of the hill's presence. Though less high than the surrounding ridges, it steadily draws the attention, at the same time navel and power-house. It is, one feels, the centre of Neolithic England.

With the framework of the Ridgeway road, Windmill Hill camp, the long barrow and the man-made hill in mind, one is ready to approach

100. Silbury Hill, the largest man-made hill in Europe, built around 2600 BC. It is a round cone, with a flattened top, built of chalk and now covered with grass. The ancient Ridgeway road runs along the top of the hill on the right of the picture.

the circle complex itself. On the top of the rise to the east of Silbury
Hill, one of the key crossing-points of England can be found. The old
Great West Road crosses the ancient Ridgeway there, and in one angle
of the crossing is the site called the Sanctuary. The plans of the vanished structures there are now indicated by concrete markers in the
ground. At about the same time as Silbury Hill was started, a small
circle of posts was erected at the Sanctuary. Soon afterwards, this was
surrounded by a larger circle of upright timbers. All this earlier work
was removed, perhaps in about 2400 BC, and a broader wooden structure still was built, with perhaps five concentric rings of posts. One or
more of these three structures of timber may have been roofed over,
rather than being open to the sky, but that is not established. Finally, at
some time after the Beaker people arrived in about 2300 BC – if one

101. The surviving part of the Avenue, a double row of standing stones that ran from
the Sanctuary, beside the Ridgeway, for a mile and a half to the Avebury rings.

judges by the pottery fragments found – two concentric circles of standing stones were built at the Sanctuary. One was within the area of the wooden circles, the other of much larger diameter. From the northwest side of these circles, the long avenue of two standing stone rows wound a mile and a half over the side of the ridge, down to the valley and on as far as the circular embankment and ditch containing the largest circle of standing stones ever built. Much of the Avenue has vanished now, but it is good to follow its course.

The road, down the hill to West Kennet village and then right to

Fig. 38. Plan of the Avebury henge and stone circles indicating the original design and the positions of known stones, whether standing or destroyed. The plan omits all modern roads and buildings.

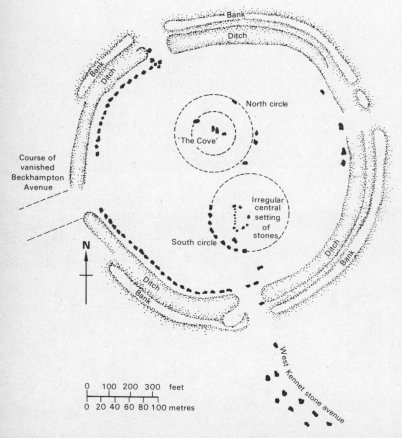

102. Avebury. The southern part of the outer great stone circle, with some stones of the Avenue visible through the gap in the embankment.

Avebury, follows the former route of the Avenue fairly closely. Before Avebury is reached, a surviving stretch of the two rows runs parallel with the minor road, giving a feeling of what this great processional route was like. Several facing pairs of stones are roughly pillar-shaped and broadly massive, as if male and female. Along the way a number of pits containing ritual debris and shards have been found. Then the high embankment is reached, itself an earthwork to compare with Silbury, and the stones of the great circle inside the bank appear. Some of these stones are enormous – huge rough boulders of Sarsen brought down to the valley from the Marlborough Downs on the far side of the Ridgeway (where many similar rocks still lie scattered on the land).

Avebury's outer circle and banks were either laid out with great complexity or else the exactness of this ring was not significant to the builders. Since the two (largely destroyed) inner circles are almost exactly round, it would seem more likely that the outer one was intended as a symbolic or sacred enclosure on a monumental scale rather than an astronomical instrument. The banks and ditches are almost complete, while many of the big stones remain on the western side. The two inner circles, themselves larger than any other except the Ring of Brodgar in Orkney (which is of the same size and approximate date, perhaps indicating a link) were clearly the ritual and perhaps astronomical centres of the place. Only a few stones of the inner rings remain in place, but two of the three huge monoliths within the northern circle – which originally formed a U-shaped setting now called the Cove – are still there. This inner northern circle had two concentric rings, one of thirty stones and the other of twelve. Inside the southern inner circle of thirty stones there was a strange irregular setting of small stones (whose function may have been astronomical but has not yet been deciphered) and a tall central pillar on a spot later used for a maypole. To judge from pottery found in the embankment, the whole vast concept was realized during the centuries on either side of 2500 BC by Neolithic people, for only the later layers contained beaker fragments. The whole enclosure has been seen as a vast pantheon temple, with people from far places performing their own rites there at special festivals in one or other of the inner circles (Burl 1976, 330).

The houses of the pretty village of Avebury straggle into the perimeters of these circles now, while high trees and the surrounding hills add to the beauty of the site. The church, the Elizabethan manor house and the attractive little museum all lie respectfully outside the great circle's banks. People often have very intense and varied feelings here.

103. The northern part of the outer circle, with its henge of ditch and bank, all built around 2500 B C.

Oddly, some of the most rationalist feel great unease: others have more uplifting experiences. Walk clockwise around the outer embankment in silence and you will feel in harmony with the earth and the sky.

The surviving stones of Avebury are fairly safe from damage today. It was not always so. The monuments were unknown to western civilization until John Aubrey and later William Stukeley publicized it in the 1660s and 1740s. Later in Stukeley's century, many stones were destroyed by farmers, and it is only through his drawings that we know that there was another avenue to the west of the great circle. This ran along the lane past the church, curved southwards through the fields beyond (where just two enormous stones survive) and ended near what is now the Beckhampton roundabout. Since Stukeley's drawing, many of its stoneholes have been found. The overall plan of the Avebury works of the high period at the end of the Neolithic age was therefore a

243

long serpentine avenue, with the henged circles in the middle of the curve and the hill of Silbury within its arms. The plan is open to many interpretations on various planes – symbolic, spiritual or practical. Both avenues go near streams, which may be significant. What is clear from the many later round barrows in the surrounding country is that it remained a sacred area long after its builders gave way to the warlike people of the age of metal.

104. The Cove, Avebury. Two of the three huge stones which stood at the centre of the northern inner circle (which consisted of two concentric rings). The Cove formed a U-shaped pattern, with its open side towards the midsummer sunrise.

105. Adam and Eve, the only surviving stones of the second avenue which originally ran westward from the Avebury circles. Both avenues were built at the same period as the circles.

Like Avebury – which lies twenty miles to the north – Stonehenge is best seen in the context of its surrounding country and nearby monuments. As the map shows, there are at least three long barrows within a radius of a mile and a half from the main ring, indicating that the area was an important one several hundred years before the first known work of 2800 BC at the site of the great stone circle. Two miles to the north-west, the causewayed camp of Durrington Walls (perhaps the home of the people who built Stonehenge) has been excavated and revealed some complicated timber structures which date from 2400 BC

Fig. 39. Outline map showing the earthworks and megalithic monuments in the area around Stonehenge, Wiltshire, England.

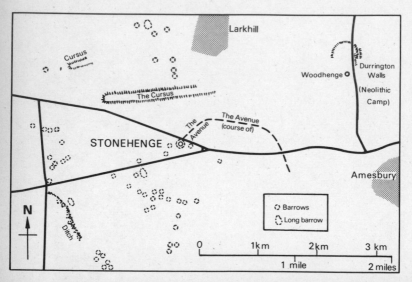

106. Stonehenge and its surrounding countryside from the west.

– right at the end of the Neolithic period before the Beaker people imposed themselves. Outside the southern end of Durrington Walls, concrete stumps in a field beside the A345 road mark the tree-trunk rings of Woodhenge, a monument built in 2300 BC after the infiltration of the metal-using Beaker folk – the pottery found there is a mixture of theirs and of the older Neolithic type. It was to be another three centuries before the Beaker people started to close up the long barrows and to end the use of the causewayed camps. But they continued to regard the Stonehenge area as holy, for the map shows that the country is covered with the small round barrows in which they buried their dead, usually singly.

At the centre of all this is Stonehenge itself, with its outlying earth-works. Half a mile to the north of the circle, a man-made depression in the land runs almost east–west for over a mile. This is the Cursus, one of several such earthwork monuments traced in Wessex. It has been demonstrated that they have significant alignments for astronomy (see Wood 1978, 102) but they must have had other more elusive purposes too. Processions and athletic races have been suggested. But the link which comes to mind repeatedly in many parts of Europe is the possible metaphysical use of long aligned enclosures, especially those running about east–west. The stone rows of Carnac, the long raised enclosures of Denmark, the ramps at Monte d'Accoddi in Sardinia, the line of monuments at Wéris in Belgium, avenues of standing stones in many countries – all suggest places where perhaps mankind could project some force into the heavens or, more likely, where the earth could receive some beneficial energy from the sky. Some will find such a notion absurd nowadays, but it fits in with an overall pattern of what megalithic monuments were for, which we shall bring together in the conclusions of this book.

A visit to the Stonehenge great circle itself again starts best with a walk through its surroundings. To the north-east of the stones, the slightly raised ground of the Avenue can be seen to run through the fields after passing the standing stone called the Heel Stone and cross-ing the road – after a few hundred metres it swings around to the right (though most of it has been ploughed flat over the centuries) and ends by running south-south-east to the banks of the Avon river. To walk the Avenue would be the proper approach to Stonehenge, but it cannot be done across crop-bearing fields today. At least let us look for-ward to the implementation of the government scheme to remove the A344 road past the circle and build a distant car-park so that visitors

107. Stonehenge and the Heel Stone.

approach the circle at the end of a long walk.

After entering the field in which Stonehenge stands, it is valuable to walk in a wide clockwise circle as far away from the stones as the fences permit. The impression that the site is flattish disappears as this walk progresses – from the south-east the stones vanish behind the brow of the hill, while from the west one sees that the monument is on a lower level. At this point it is also evident that this is another instance of the type of megalithic site we have noticed in many places – the circle stands on the slope of a gentle ridge, with the skyline hills cradling the valley beneath it. The scale is quite different from that of Filitosa in Corsica or the Knebel dolmen in Denmark, but the basic visible pattern of the land is the same and the great circle sits harmoniously in its surroundings.

Stonehenge as it survives in part today is the result of several stages of building and radical rebuilding over a 1000 years or more. Professor

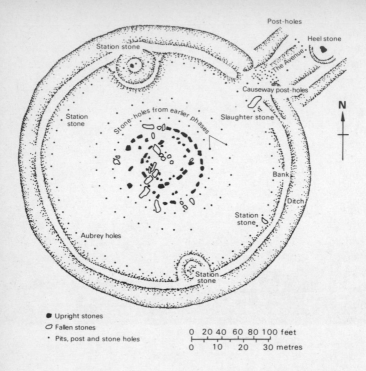

Fig. 40. Plan of Stonehenge with its surrounding henge, showing the stones of the present monument and the holes detected which show the plans of the earlier stages.

R. J. C. Atkinson, the archaeologist who has done most work there, has divided the building into five stages or sub-stages (Atkinson 1960). These are conveniently clear, so we shall follow them here without necessarily accepting all of Atkinson's conclusions.

The earliest work which archaeologists have traced on the site appears to date from around 2800 BC. This is six centuries after Newgrange in Ireland but at the start of the great period of late Neolithic building in Britain, from Orkney to Bodmin Moor. At Stonehenge this work is called Phase 1 and it did not apparently involve a stone circle. The henge itself – the ring of banks and ditch around the enclosure, broken by one level causeway – has been dated to this stage, as has the circle of fifty-six holes (called the Aubrey Holes after the antiquarian John Aubrey) just inside the bank. A number of post-holes thought to be of this phase have also been detected in the earth of the caueway, as have some empty stoneholes at the entrance through the bank. Finally, it is believed that the Slaughter Stone at the entrance to the embankment (originally one of an upright gateway pair), the outlying Heel Stone and a row of post-holes near it may be of this period. The monument at this first stage, therefore, was not visually impressive – it seems that it may well have been a working laboratory for astronomers as much as a temple. Analysis of the traces mentioned above has shown that it could have been used in this way, probably to observe the moon's movements. Many detailed interpretations have been put forward (e.g. Lockyer 1909, Trotter 1927, Hawkins 1963, 1970 and 1974, Hoyle 1966, Thom 1974 and 1975). The Heel Stone is thought to have marked a lunar alignment originally, rather than the midsummer sunrise. It seems quite possible, on the evidence of the post-holes, that it was at this first observatory of earthworks and posts that the existence of the moon's main cycle of 18.61 years was discovered by systematic observations over that period and its regularity confirmed by continuing this work for a total of six cycles. This would have been a discovery of great importance for a people to whom the moon was divine, and a considerable step towards predicting eclipses. If it happened here, that may account for the veneration of Stonehenge as a place and its later glorification in stone.

It was in about 2500 or 2400 BC that the first stone circle at Stonehenge was erected. This is known as Phase 2. The stones were not large ones – nothing to compare with the huge monoliths being erected at Avebury and Stenness at about the same time – but they were very special. These Bluestones, as they are called, were probably brought here more than 150 miles from the Prescelly Mountains in Wales. The mountain of Carn Meini at Prescelly is said to have been sacred (Burl 1976, 308). They were erected in two concentric circles whose empty stoneholes can still be traced (some of the Bluestones were later re-erected elsewhere around the present Sarsen circle, as we shall see later). It is obvious that the Bluestones had special properties, as did the recumbent stones in the Aberdeenshire circles which also came from distant places, but we do not know what those properties were. The prone Altar Stone in the centre (now under fallen Sarsens) is also from Wales, from an outcrop at Milford Haven; it probably stood upright originally.

108. Stonehenge. Detail of part of the sarsen–capped ring built in about 2100 BC, with one of the earlier and smaller Bluestones (which were brought from Wales in about 2500 BC) on the left.

At the same time as the concentric Bluestone rings were built, the four small Station Stones were erected beside the outer bank forming, as it were, the corners of a big oblong across the centre of the enclosure. Two of these stones have gone now, but their small circular ditches remain. The ditch at the Heel Stone was dug too, and the earthwork platform of the Avenue was raised – empty stoneholes run along its central axis. These works altered the basic orientation of the monument from lunar to solar, perhaps marking a shift in religious emphasis on the deities (Burl 1976, 310). Not only does the Avenue run towards the midsummer sunrise (and therefore the Heel Stone is taken to indicate that direction) but the diagonal lines across the quadrangle formed by the Station Stones (and across the stone circle's centre) point to the midwinter and midsummer risings of the sun. These stones also point to important moonrise points. It is interesting, and possibly significant, to note that only at Stonehenge's latitude could those alignments be indicated by a rectangular quadrilateral – at any other latitude the pattern of the four stones would have to be a parallelogram. This Bluestone circle and Station Stone phase was apparently the last to be built by Neolithic people.

The building stage called Phase 3-A brought about the spectacular Stonehenge which we know today. This appears to have been constructed in about 2100 BC, after the Beaker people had established their domination and brought the use of bronze. They dug up the Bluestone circles and dumped them to one side. Then they brought much larger blocks of Sarsen stone from the Marlborough Downs near the Ridgeway (where the big Avebury stones came from too). They erected the ten largest blocks in pairs to form a horseshoe pattern around the centre of the circle, each pair being capped by a horizontal Sarsen slab to form what is called a trilithon. Alexander Thom has pointed out that this horseshoe pattern in fact runs around the perimeter of an exact ellipse.

Around the horseshoe of trilithons, but inside the positions of the earlier Bluestone circles, they built a tremendous ring of Sarsen stones, each linked to the next by a big capstone so that a continuous line was formed at their topmost level.

The monument which the Beaker people achieved, much grander than any other circle except Avebury's outer ring, has several strange features. This is the only occasion when a Beaker-dominated community seems to have built on a really big scale with giant stones. The other Great Stone Circles all seem to have been built by Neolithic

109. One of the five giant trilithons of sarsen, built at Stonehenge in about 2100 B.C.

peoples, while the hundreds of Beaker circles around the British Isles are almost all small in diameter and use only medium-sized stones. Moreover, the new capstoned structure does not seem to have much astronomical use, unless the theory is accepted that the capstones were themselves used as observation points (Wood 1978, 181). Otherwise, it appears that the new temple was meant primarily to provide an overwhelmingly impressive setting for seasonal and perhaps eclipse rites, in which ritual observations of the skies may have played a part.

The alterations to Stonehenge were not finished yet. Phase 3-B, perhaps of about 1900 BC, saw a re-erection of some of the Welsh Bluestones in a wide spiral pattern around the Sarsen-capped circle (again, the stoneholes can be traced). This may have been connected with ritual dances, but whatever the function, the Bluestones were not left in that position for more than three centuries. In Phase 3-C, in around 1600 BC, they were rearranged into the present pattern within the trilithon horseshoe, and into a circle between the horseshoe and the Sarsen-capped ring (some of this circle remains, but most of it has been destroyed). No astronomical significance has been found for these settings, so again we must assume that it was the special qualities of the Bluestones that justified their use.

That brings us to the end of the stages of Stonehenge and almost to the end of the period when the British weather made observation of celestial bodies feasible. Thom pointed out, after his 1976 survey of the monument, that suitable foresight markers do exist on the Stonehenge skyline for the sort of accurate long-distance observations that were carried out elsewhere. One more piece of conjecture is unavoidable on the basis of the evidence available. If the Beaker folk started to dominate the population around Stonehenge in about 2300 BC (as indicated by the Durrington and Woodhenge finds), they may well have adopted the astronomical part of the local people's religion in order to confirm their own authority. They may also have decided, exceptionally for them, to give Stonehenge visual grandeur to assist with the transfer of the centre of authority from Avebury to this site. Furthermore, they may have become obsessed with refining their predictions of the moon's movements and of the eclipses, and so spread the hundreds of small observatory-temple circles throughout most of Britain. Observatories at different latitudes would give them more information and, as far north as Temple Wood and beyond that Callanish in Scotland, we have seen that the moon could be observed to move in patterns that could only be guessed at in Wessex or in Brittany. The thought that such an overall

pattern lay behind the spread of lunar laboratories is, however, completely speculative at present.

Mention megaliths, or even standing stones, to many people and they will ask, 'What's that?' Mention Stonehenge, and almost anyone in Britain and numerous people in continental Europe will say, 'Oh, yes – of course.' To such an extent did the designers of the monument succeed in submerging knowledge of its predecessors and contemporaries. It is to be hoped that this book will enable people to explore more of those tremendous megalithic works in almost every country of western Europe, and to see the sort of links and differences that existed between these countries 5000 years ago. Equally it must be hoped that the British authorities will care for that most famous megalithic temple as it deserves. The public must have access to it, but the millions of human feet which have tramped it in the last few decades – not to mention the fences, the concrete and the barbed wire – seem to have driven the spirit of the place far underground.

110. Stonehenge and rainbow.

Conclusions

We see the megaliths as having an outer and an inner level of meaning. The outer level, that of ritual and common knowledge, is concerned with such matters as the prosperity, fertility and well-being of the people, the land and the crops.

Within a thousand years of settling, the first farmers started to build megaliths in most parts of western Europe. The intention which lay behind the designs of megalithic shrines of all periods in the following 3000 years was to ensure the fertilization of the earth by metaphysical energies from the sky, and to maintain the cycles of growth and decline, death and rebirth, in all living things. Recurring myths of creation tell of the moment when the shaft of the male principle first pierced and fixed the floating female mound, causing heaven and earth to fly apart into their present positions. That event is symbolized in the design of the earliest kind of megalith, the rounded mound pierced by a passage to a stone chamber at its core. At such sanctuaries, positioned in special places on the earth's surface, the life-cycle of mankind was ritualized in complex ceremonies. Some of these were performed upon death and burial. At other times, in the presence of the mortal remains of previous generations, the year's important festivals were marked by rites to regenerate the land and the people gathered around the mound. The key to these rites was the catching of a particular moment in the cycles of the sun or moon or even an individual star. At such moments and in such sacred places, mankind could by appropriate ritual bring together the forces of sky and earth to harmonize with each other. And each reassertion of this harmony could nourish the soil as well as the human spirit.

In these early chambered mounds built from 4500 BC onwards, the most beneficial moment of the year seems to have been sunrise at the midwinter solstice, when the sun ended his long autumn waning and was in some sense reborn for the new year. Another special instant was probably the sunrise at the spring or autumn equinox, turning-points in the sun's progress through the annual cycle. The entrance passages of most mounds face the point on the horizon where the sun rises on one or other of these days, so that its first light would penetrate and illuminate the chamber within.

Later, the megalith builders developed designs which would focus on other important moments of the year. The long raised enclosures, built after 3500 BC, called long barrows in Britain but other names elsewhere, sometimes point to the equinoctial sunrise, sometimes to the midsummer sunrise. As time went on, midsummer perhaps became increasingly important and more monuments were oriented towards it, towards the benefits given by the sun in his prime rather than his midwinter infancy. The celebration of this day in the year has survived throughout Europe.

Soon after 3000 BC, the chief events of the moon's phases became as significant as the sun's movements in the new works of the megalith builders, suggesting the start of a period when her powers were found of renewed value – for the moon's influence had been great in earlier times too. Her movements were more difficult to predict than the sun's and for more than a thousand years mankind built a range of increasingly complicated observatories for these studies – great earthworks, alignments, fans and circles. Most of these have markers which indicate such important horizon positions as the farthest north or south rising and setting points of the moon – sometimes together with sun and star rise markers – but others show much more abstruse purposes. These were increasingly refined attempts to predict the exact moment of eclipses of sun or moon.

The reason for all this complex astronomy was not just the advancement of scientific knowledge, for only small parts of the lines and circles could be used for observation or prediction. The aim of the huge monuments themselves, and the point of their complex geometry, was to draw the power of a special instant to the people gathered at the end of the stone rows or within the great stone rings. For after each death of the sun or moon through eclipse, there would come a rebirth of the light in a moment that carried high spiritual force for the people assembled at the sacred place after long preparation, a moment when their response could amplify that power and help to feed its benefits over the land and into the soil through countless outlying menhirs.

On another level, the megalithic monuments may be seen as engines of transformation. This inner level of meaning, the esoteric, deals with the work of personal regeneration.

Looking again at the account of the creation we have referred to so often, we have the images of the primordial waters, the mound taking shape upon them, and all the ensuing drama. Each of us formed and grew, floating in those waters. Each of us emerged after a strenuous, convulsing passage from the primeval mound. To establish our identity, we create, and assert duality – the I and the Other. Each of us has struggled physically and emotionally, to emerge from the undifferentiated state. This questing, differentiating consciousness is the mode through which we strive to know the world around us, to give coherence to that knowledge, and to find our orientation within it.

With that 'separate' consciousness, we carry the original wound, our sense of less and alienation from the universal source. When we no longer experience ourselves as one with life, we are at odds with it, and we dramatise the struggle unceasingly. We project our inner conflict about that loss onto the world around us. Survival and achievement seem to depend on dominating, or resisting, or manipulating aspects of ourselves we are uncomfortable with; the people we love, and those we work with; our physical environment; the weather; the planet itself – that very Earth which once we trusted to nourish and support us.

So the inner work may be seen as a process of rediscovering the unity which underlies our separation, and learning to open in trust again. We can become conscious of those things we had forgotten or hidden. We can own our conflicts, quite literally, recognising that they are all within us, and that we alone have the power to resolve them, if we so choose.

And this requires, not that we learn to do things differently, but simply that we give up the defences we invented out of fear and resistance – layer by layer. Each step is a death of sorts, the more painful as we impede it, which has to be fully experienced before we are reborn freer and lighter.

We have a great deal to learn from visiting and studying the megaliths which remain to us from a time when men apparently lived at peace with each other, needing no weapons, in harmony with nature.

These monuments, in their forms – the womb-like mounds, the pillar menhirs, the great temple-observatories: in their orientation – first on the rising of the new-born sun at the dead of winter, then on the other turning points of the year, and of much longer cycles: in their rituals – the ecstatic dance, the trance-sleep of healing and illumination – recall us to the cyclical rhythms of life.

These great structures were built to enhance very special places on the earth's surface, where a force or current works to make this expansion of consciousness more intense. Stones were chosen for their unique properties, which in some way amplify these forces, and then arranged in a plan designed to focus them very specifically. They may encourage us in our labyrinthine journeys into darkness. Each of these journeys is a kind of death, and we can find in the megaliths reassurance of our coming back into the light, reborn, transformed, so that in ourselves we resolve and integrate light and dark, masculine and feminine, each of us the Axis Mundi, joining Heaven and Earth again.

Suggestions for Further Research

We are strongly aware of the gaps in our knowledge about the megaliths. Some of those could not be made good by the techniques available at present, and some mysteries may be best left as such. Other gaps could be filled, and perhaps have been, without our being aware of the research.

As far as particular places are concerned, the completion of the partly done excavation around Monte d'Accoddi in Sardinia is the most pressing need. It has already revealed what seems a fascinating meeting-point of the western megalithic tradition with eastern influences and the unexplored part shows some mysterious features above ground. As regards archaeology in general, sensitive excavations of unspoiled stone circle sites and the forecourts of chambered mounds in Denmark, Scotland and Ireland have already given clues about the non-funerary rituals; much more knowledge is needed. On another point, it seems almost unbelievable that we have been able to trace few megalithic monuments in Iberia except chambered mounds and none in southern Germany except menhirs – more fieldwork may well reveal a greater variety.

A plotting of all chambered mounds and dolmens in Europe, with radiocarbon or thermoluminescence dates and the direction in which their entrances face, would be a major undertaking but would tell us a great deal about the geographical spread and the chronology of the cult of the midwinter sunrise, as well as other significant directions. A similar plotting of all long barrows and related raised enclosures, with orientations and dates where known, should reveal much about those monuments – a comparison of these with a plot of all alignments (large and small) with orientations and dates, may show a strong link between many aligned monuments from different parts of Europe. The task of plotting all single standing stones in Europe is perhaps too vast to contemplate at present, but an important start could be made by plotting all menhirs of considerable size, especially those which stand in solitary positions from the Outer Hebrides to Leipzig and to central France or further. From the available evidence it is impossible even to guess what sort of patterns would emerge from an accurate plot of this sort: the work would not require an archaeologist to do it, since any painstaking researcher could compile the positions in time.

The same could be said of three other Europe-wide plots which are needed. One of these should be of all the man-made and (more common) apparently man-carved hills which can be traced, keeping a record of their shapes. The second would be of monuments which are set out in units of 2.72 feet, Professor Thom's megalithic yard, in continental Europe. The other could be of all known long-distance straight alignments of monuments, of the sort widely reported in England and Germany. The work of the small group of dowsers who have reported the overground charged lines mentioned in the introduction needs confirmation by other dowsers, while the dowsers' underground patterns found at a few stone circles could well be confirmed or improved at other circles and at megalithic sites of all sorts throughout Europe. This dowsing work has perhaps only just started to touch on the information which it alone may be able to provide.

Other work is needed on the properties of stone. It seems unlikely that Neolithic people would go to extreme trouble to obtain particular stones for particular positions merely for superstitious reasons. Different types of stone obviously have different constituents, yet nothing relevant to archaeological knowledge seems to have been researched. The properties of quartz, many of which are known, might make a good starting-point – for many megaliths are of stone which contains much quartz. Another rewarding approach may be research into the particular qualities of the Welsh Bluestones at Stonehenge and of other megaliths known to have been brought from a distance for reasons other than the simple availability of large strong rocks.

As regards megalithic astronomy, Alexander Thom and his family have analysed some of the possibilities of most British sites and of the Carnac monuments. Similar work is now needed at the aligned enclosures of Holland, Germany and Denmark, at Wéris in Belgium, at the alignments of Corsica, the circles and mounds in Sardinia and the temples of Malta. Only in Belgium and Malta have we heard of any investigation at all in progress, yet evidence of the presence or absence of such studies in Neolithic societies could tell us much about the extent of contacts between communities in the period from 3000 to 1500 BC.

Short Glossary

Alignment or Alinement – A row of standing stones.

Anta – Portuguese word for a dolmen.

Avenue – As applied to megaliths, two rows of standing stones.

Barrow – A mound of earth, which may be of various shapes (long, round, bell, disk, etc.), over a chamber.

Beaker – Funnel, Bell, etc. – A pot with a rounded lower part narrowing to a neck and then swelling to a flared lip (see Fig. 2). Various shapes of beaker are associated with particular cultures: e.g. the funnel beaker with the late Neolithic people who occupied southern Scandinavia, the Netherlands, northern Germany and Poland: the bell beaker with the Early Bronze Age people who seem to have colonized large areas of Europe after 2500 BC and are often called simply 'the Beaker people'.

Betyl – A small pillar of stone, thought to have been a venerated object.

Cairn – A mound of stones, sometimes covering a chamber. In some countries the term is used to describe any such mound, whether it is made of stones or earth or both.

Capstone – A large stone laid across the top of other stones, usually to form the roof of a chamber or dolmen.

Chambered Mound – An earth mound or barrow with a chamber, usually of stones, inside it.

Cist – A box-like chamber of stone slabs, usually smaller than chambers described as dolmens.

Corbelled – In megalithic structure, a roof formed by horizontal layers of stone which overlap each other as they rise and are closed off at the top.

Cromlec or Cromlech – In France, a ring of standing stones. In Wales a dolmen.

Cueva – Spanish word for a chambered mound.

Cupmark – *Cup-and-Ring Mark* – A cupmark is a rounded depression carved into the face of a stone. Cup-and-Ring marks are concentric rings carved around a cupmark, often with another line penetrating from outside the rings to the cupmark in the centre.

Cyclopean – A type of drystone building consisting of successive layers of large irregular stones fitting closely to each other and forming a wall.

Dolmen – A chamber formed by megaliths. Dolmens often stand by themselves today. Most were originally the core of a chambered mound, and many are still within their mounds. The term dolmen is regarded as inexact and outdated by some archaeologists, but is valued and established among most other people.

Dysser – Danish term for megalithic chambered structures in general, including the raised enclosures called Long Dysser, the dolmens encircled by stone rings called Round Dysser, and the chambered mounds of the passage grave type.

Enclosure – A general term used to describe any area of ground bordered by rows of standing stones or earth embankments, often for sacred purposes.

Gallery Grave – Archaeological term for a megalithic chamber consisting of one long space, as against the passage plus broader chamber arrangement of a 'passage grave'. A gallery grave is called an *allée couverte* in French.

Grooved Ware – A type of decorated pottery made by some Neolithic people in England before the appearance of Beaker pottery.

Henge – An enclosure usually formed by a roughly circular earthwork ditch and bank. Henges often had circles of standing stones or timbers within the earthworks.

Hunebed (Hun's Bed) – A type of dolmen found in the Netherlands, consisting of a row of rough trilithons which enclosed a long narrow chamber.

Hünengrab (Huns' Grave) – The German equivalent of the Hunebed of the Netherlands, also called a *Steingrab* (Stone grave).

Hypogeum – A large underground chamber.

Kerb – In archaeology, a term used to describe a ring of large stones around the bottom edge of a mound.

Megalith – A great stone, often used loosely to mean a monument built of great stones.

Menhir – A solitary standing stone, usually of great size and carved to a particular shape. In French, the word is normally used to describe any standing stone which does not support anything.

Mesolithic – An archaeological term for the middle part of the Stone Age, before the settled farming of the Neolithic Age.

Midden – An ancient rubbish dump, usually of household refuse.

Naveta – A form of burial-chamber found in Menorca, built of cyclopean stonework and in the shape of a flat-sterned boat turned upside down.

Neolithic – An archaeological term for the late part of the Stone Age, during which most megaliths were built, when settled farming had replaced the earlier nomadic and hunting way of life.

Nuraghe – A round tower made of cyclopean masonry, sometimes extended into a complex of such towers. Hundreds of nuraghi can be found in Sardinia, where they were built by a late megalithic people whose 'nuragic' culture is named after them.

Orthostat – A slab of stone set upright in the ground, often supporting the roof or capstone of a dolmen.

Passage Grave – Archaeological term for a megalithic chamber consisting of a passage leading to a broader space (often a dolmen), as against the long chamber – without narrow passage – of a 'gallery grave'.

Radiocarbon – Carbon 14, a substance found in all living material, which gradually disappears at a known rate from the moment life ceases. Measurement of the proportion of radiocarbon in ancient material therefore enables it to be dated.

Recumbent – Lying down. In megalithic monuments the term is particularly applied to circles of standing stones in Scotland and Ireland which have several upright megaliths and one larger stone lying along the circumference.

Revetment – A kerb (q.v.) of large stones retaining the lower edge of a mound.

Sanctuary – As used in this book, a monument of megaliths or earthworks which apparently had a sacred function.

Setting – A vague archaeological term for any arrangement of large stones which does not fit into one of the named megalithic categories.

Stazzone – Sardinian word for a dolmen.

Talayot – The equivalent in the Balearics of the nuraghe tower of Sardinia. The talayots were probably built by conquering Sardinian people and their Balearic culture is known as 'talayotic'.

Taula – The great standing stones, with a shallow capstone, which formed the centre of the sanctuaries of the talayotic people in Menorca. The word *taula* means a table in Catalan.

Temple – As applied to megalithic structures, a religious building which does not fit into any of the widespread named types of sacred structure.

Thermoluminescence – A constituent of all pottery that has been fired, which decays at a known rate. This enables the pottery material to be analysed and a date given for its firing.

Tholos – A Greek word for a corbelled (q.v.) roof structure.

Torrean (Torréen) – The French term for the builders of cyclopean stone towers in Corsica, who were probably the same people as the nuraghe builders (q.v.) of Sardinia.

Trilithon – An arrangement of two megaliths set upright int the ground, with a third placed across the tops of both.

Tumulus – A Latin word which was at one time used for a prehistoric mound or barrow.

Wattle and Daub – An ancient form of walling, consisting of interwoven branches infilled with clay and various other binding substances.

References and Select Bibliography

Almagro, M. and Arribas, A., *El Poblado y la Necropolis Megaliticos de Los Millares* (Madrid 1963)

Anati, E., *The Camonica Valley* (London 1964)

Anderson, J. R. L., *The Oldest Road – an exploration of the Ridgeway* (London 1975)

Ashbee, Paul, *The Earthen Long Barrow in Britain* (London 1970)

Atkinson, R. J. C., *Stonehenge and Avebury, and neighbouring monuments* (London 1959)

Atkinson, R. J. C., *Stonehenge* (London 1960)

Behrend, Michael, *The Landscape Geometry of Southern Britain* (Institute of Geomantic Research, Cambridge 1975)

Bennett, F. J., *On the Meridional Position of Megaliths in Kent compared with those of Wilts* (reprinted Cambridge 1978, originally published in the South-Eastern Naturalist 1904)

Bord, Janet and Colin, *Mysterious Britain* (London 1972)

Bowen, Collin, *see* Fowler P. J. (ed.)

Branigan, Keith, *Prehistoric Britain – an illustrated survey* (Bourne End 1976)

Brea, Bernabo, *Sicily* (London 1957)

Brothwell, D. and Higgs, E. (eds), *Science in Archaeology* (London 1963) including 'Dating Pottery by Thermoluminescence' by E. T. Hall.

Brown, P. Lancaster. *Megaliths and Masterminds* (London 1979)

Burl, Aubrey, *The Stone Circles of the British Isles* (New Haven and London 1976)

Butterworth, E. A. S., *The Tree at the Navel of the Earth* (Berlin 1970)

Cambry, *Monuments Celtiques ou recherches sur le Culte des Pierres* (1805)

Charpentier, Louis, *The Mysteries of Chartres Cathedral* (Paris 1966; London 1972)

Childe, V. Gordon, *Skara Brae – a Pictish village in Orkney* (London 1931)

Childe, V. Gordon, *Prehistoric Communities of the British Isles* (London 1940)

Childe, V. Gordon, *Ancient Dwellings at Skara Brae* (Edinburgh 1950)

Childe, V. Gordon, *The Dawn of European Civilization* (London, revised edition 1957)

Clarke, D. V., *The Neolithic Village at Skara Brae, Orkney – 1972–73 excavations, an interim report* (Edinburgh 1976)

Coffey, George, *New Grange and other incised tumuli in Ireland* (reprinted Poole 1977, originally published 1912)

Collins, Desmond (ed.), *The Origins of Europe* (London 1975)

Cox, John, *A Guide to the Compass* (limited edition London 1978)

Crawford, O. G. S., *The Eye Goddess* (New York 1957)

Critchlow, Keith (ed.), *Earth Mysteries – a study in patterns* (London 1977) including contributions by the editor 'The Cosmology of Stone Circles'; by A., A. S. and A. S. Thom 'Stonehenge'; by J. and C. Bord 'Ancient Sites – Alive or Dead?'; by T. Graves 'Earth Energies'; by J. Michell 'The Old Straight Track' and others.

Czaja, Michael, *Gods of Myth and Stone – phallicism in Japanese folk religion* (New York and Tokyo 1974)

Dames, Michael, *The Silbury Treasure – the Great Goddess rediscovered* (London 1976)

Dames, Michael, *The Avebury Cycle* (London 1977)

Daniel, Glyn, *The Prehistoric Chamber Tombs of England and Wales* (Cambridge 1950)

Daniel, Glyn, *The Megalith Builders of Western Europe* (London 1958)

Daniel, Glyn, *The Prehistoric Chamber Tombs of France* (London 1960)

Daniel, Glyn, *Megaliths in History* (London 1972)

Davidson, H. Ellis, *see* Gelling, P.

Diodorus Siculus (fl. 60–20 BC), *Bibliotheca Historica*

Dyer, James, *Discovering Archaeology in Denmark* (Aylesbury 1972)

Eitel, E. J., *Feng Shui* (1873, republished Cambridge 1973)

Evans, J. D., *Malta* (London 1959)

Evans, J. G., *The Environment of Early Man in the British Isles* (London 1975)

Fergusson, James, *Rude Stone Monuments in All Countries – their age and uses* (London 1872)

Fowler, P. J. (ed.), *Recent Work in Rural Archaeology* (Bradford-on-Avon 1975) with contributions by the editor on 'Continuity in the Landscape of Wiltshire, Somerset and Gloucestershire'; by Collin Bowen on 'Pattern and Interpretation: a view of the Wessex Landscape'; by Roger Mercer on 'Settlement, Farming and Environment in South West England'; by Geoffrey Wainwright on 'Religion and Settlement in Wessex 3000–1700 BC'; by Euan MacKie on 'The Brochs of Scotland', and others.

Fowles, John, *Islands* (London 1978)

Gelling, P. and Davidson, H. Ellis, *The Chariot of the Sun – rites and symbols of the northern bronze age* (London 1969)

Gerlach, Kurt, 'Holy or Functional Lines over Bohemia' (1942) and 'Ley Lines through Germany' (1943) in *Central European Geomancy* (Cambridge 1976) edited by Nigel Pennick.

Gimbutas, Marija, *The Gods and Goddesses of Old Europe 7000–3500 BC* (London 1974)

Glob, P. V., *Danish Prehistoric Monuments* (London 1971)

Gordon, E. O., *Prehistoric London – its mounds and circles* (London 1932)

Graves, Tom., *Needles of Stone* (London 1978)

Grinsell, Leslie V., *Some Aspects of the Folklore of Prehistoric Monuments* (London 1937)

Grinsell, Leslie V., *Barrow, Pyramid and Tomb – ancient burial customs* (London 1975)

Grinsell, Leslie V., *Folklore of Prehistoric Sites in Britain* (Newton Abbot and London 1976)

Grosjean, Roger, *Filitosa et son Contexte Archéologique* (Paris 1961)

Grosjean, Roger, *Filitosa – haut lieu de la Corse préhistorique* (Strasbourg and Corsica 1975)

Guido, Margaret, *Sardinia* (London 1963)

Guido, Margaret, *Sicily: an Archaeological Guide* (London 1967)

Guido, Margaret, *Southern Italy: an Archaeological Guide* (London 1972)

Hadingham, Evan, *Ancient Carvings in Britain: a Mystery* (London 1974)

Hadingham, Evan, *Circles and Standing Stones* (London 1975)

Hall, E. T., 'Dating Pottery by Thermoluminescence', *see* Brothwell (ed.).

Harbison, Peter, *Guide to the National Monuments of Ireland* (Dublin 1970)

Harbison, Peter, *The Archaeology of Ireland* (London 1976)

Hawkes, Jacquetta, *A Guide to the Prehistoric and Roman Monuments in England and Wales* (London 1951, revised 1973)

Hawkins, G. S., *Stonehenge Decoded* (London 1966)

Heinsch, Josef, 'The Sacred Geometrical Meaning of Prehistoric Orientation' (1937) in *Central European Geomancy* (Cambridge 1976) edited by Nigel Pennick.

Helm, P. J., *Exploring Prehistoric England* (London 1971)

Henshall, A. S., *The Chambered Tombs of Scotland I* (Edinburgh 1963)

Henshall, A. S., *The Chambered Tombs of Scotland II* (Edinburgh 1972)

Hodson, F. R. (ed.), *The Place of Astronomy in the Ancient World* – a joint symposium of The Royal Society and The British Academy (Oxford 1974)

Hoyle, Fred, 'Stonehenge: an Eclipse Predictor' in *Nature*, Vol. 211, pp. 454–6, 1966

Irwin, John, Lecture series on the Stupa given at the Victoria and Albert Museum, London, in 1978

Irwin, John. 'Asokan Pillars: a reassessment of the evidence. Part IV – Symbolism' in the *Burlington Magazine*, vol. CXVIII, November 1976.

Irwin, John, 'The Stupa and the Cosmic Axis: the Archaeological Evidence' in Taddei, M.(ed) *Proceedings of 4th International Conference of South Asian Archaeologists* (Naples 1979)

Jazdzewski, Konrad, *Poland* (London 1965)

Jenny, Hans, *Cymatics – the structure and dynamics of waves and vibrations* (Basel and London 1967)

Jones, Inigo, *The Most Notable Antiquity of Great Britain vulgarly called Stonehenge* (London 1655)

Klindt-Jensen, Ole, *Denmark before the Vikings* (London 1957)

Knöll, Heinz, *Die Nordwestdeutsche Tiefstichkeramik und Ihre Stellung im Nord – und Mitteleuropäischen Neolithikum* (Munster 1959)

Kühn, Herbert, *Rock Pictures of Europe* (London 1956)

Laet, Sigfried J. de, *The Low Countries* (London 1958)

Lamb, H. H., 1974, *see* Hodson, F. R. (ed.)

Leisner, Georg and Vera, *Die Megalithgräber der Iberischen Halbinsel* (Berlin 1943 and 1956)

Levy, G. R., *The Gate of Horn* (London 1946)

Lilliu, Giovanni, *Scultura della Sardegna Nuragica* (Venice 1956)

Lockyer, Norman J., *Stonehenge and other British Stone Monuments Astronomically Considered* (London 1906)

Lukis, William C., *The Prehistoric Stone Monuments of the British Isles* (London 1885)

MacKie, Euan, *The Megalith Builders* (Oxford 1977). References in the text to 'MacKie 1977' refer to this work

MacKie, Euan, *Science and Society in Prehistoric Britain* (London 1977)

MacKie, Euan, *see also* Fowler, P. J. (ed.)

Maclagan, David, *Creation Myths – man's introduction to the world* (London 1977)

MacRitchie, David, *The Testimony of Tradition* (London 1890)

Mahé, Abbé, *Essai sur les Antiquités du Morbihan* (1825)

Maringer, Johannes, *The Gods of Prehistoric Man* (London 1960)

Matthews, W. H., *Mazes and Labyrinths – their history and development* (London 1922, republished New York 1970)

Mayassis, S. *Architecture Religion Symbolisme – Origines, Formation et Evolution de l'Architecture* (Athens 1964 and 1966)

Mercer, Roger, *see* Fowler, P. J. (ed.)

Michell, John, *The View over Atlantis* (London 1969)

Michell, John, *City of Revelation* (London 1972)

Michell, John, *The Old Stones of Land's End* (London 1974)

Michell, John, *The Earth Spirit* (London 1975)

Michell, John, *A Little History of Astro-archaeology* (London 1977)

Munksgaard, Elisabeth, *Denmark: an Archaeological Guide* (London 1970)

Neumann, Erich, *The Great Mother – an analysis of the archetype* (London 1955)

Neustupny, E. and J., *Czechoslovakia* (London 1961)

Pallottino, M., *La Sardegna Nuragica* (Rome 1950)
Peet, T. E., *The Stone and Bronze Ages in Italy* (London 1909)
Pennick, Nigel, *Geomancy* (Cambridge 1973)
Pericot Garcia, L., *The Balearic Islands* (London 1972)
Piggott, Stuart, *Neolithic Cultures of the British Isles* (Cambridge 1954)
Piggott, Stuart, *Ancient Europe – from the beginnings of agriculture to classical antiquity* (Edinburgh 1965 and 1973)
Ponting, Gerald and Margaret. *The Standing Stones of Callanish* (Stornaway 1977)
Purce, Jill, *The Mystic Spiral – Journey of the Soul* (London 1974)

Renfrew, Colin, *Before Civilization – the radiocarbon revolution and prehistoric Europe* (London 1973)
Renfrew, Colin (ed.), *British Prehistory – a new outline* (London 1974)
Ridley, Michael, *The Megalithic Art of the Maltese Islands* (Poole 1971)
Ritchie, Anna and Graham, *The Ancient Monuments of Orkney* (Edinburgh 1978)
Roberts, Anthony, *Atlantean Traditions in Ancient Britain* (Llanfynydd, Carmarthen 1974)
Roche, Denis, *Carnac – Le Megalithisme – Archeologie/Typologie/Histoire/Mythologie* (Paris 1969)
Rollando, Y., *Les Iles de Gavrinis et d'ErLannic – leur monuments* (Vannes, no date)
Roscher, W. H., *Omphalosstudien* (Leipzig 1913)
Ross, A., *Pagan Celtic Britain* (1967)
Rouzic, Zacharie le, *Carnac – les monuments megalithiques, destination, age* (Quimper 1897 and subsequent editions, recent editions updated by M. Jacq)
Rouzic, Zacharie le, *Les Monuments megalithiques du Morbihan – causes de leur restauration* (Le Mans 1939)

Saint-Hilaire, Paul de, *L'Ardenne Mysterieuse* (Brussels 1976)
Savory, H. N., *Spain and Portugal* (London 1968)
Schrickel, W., *Westeuropäische Elemente im Neolithik Grabbau Mitteldeutschlands* (1966)
Schwenk, Theodor, *Sensitive Chaos – the creation of flowing forms in water and air* (London 1965)

Scouëzec, Gwenc'hlan le, *Guide de la Bretagne Mysterieuse* (Paris 1976)

Screeton, Paul, *Quicksilver Heritage – the mystic leys, their legacy of ancient wisdom* (Wellingborough 1974)

Shapley, H. (ed.), *Climatic Change* (Cambridge 1953)

Sikes, Wirt, *British Goblins – Welsh folk-lore, fairy mythology, legends and traditions* (London, 1880, republished Wakefield 1973)

Somerville, H. B., 'Instances of Orientations in Prehistoric Monuments of the British Isles', in *Archaeologia*, Vol. 73, pp. 193–224, 1923

Sprockhoff, Ernst, *Atlas der Megalithgräber Deutschlands* (3 vols. Schleswig-Holstein 1966; Mecklenburg and Brandenburg 1967; Niedersachsen and Westphalia 1975) (985 numbered graves)

Sprockhoff, Ernst, *Die Nordische Megalithkultur* (Berlin and Leipzig 1938)

Stenberger, M., *Sweden* (London)

Stern, Philip van Doren, *Prehistoric Europe* (London 1970)

Stukeley, William, *Stonehenge* (London 1740)

Stukeley, William, *Avebury* (London 1763)

Teudt, Wilhelm, *Germanische Heiligtümer* (Jena 1929)

Thom, Alexander, *Megalithic Sites in Britain* (Oxford 1967)

Thom, Alexander, *Megalithic Lunar Observatories* (Oxford 1971 and 1973)

Thom, Alexander and A. S. *Megalithic Remains in Britain and Brittany* (Oxford 1979). This book includes the important studies of Carnac, Orkney, Avebury and Stonehenge by the Thoms which have appeared in the *Journal for the History of Astronomy* since 1971. (Thom, October 1971, February 1972, October 1972, June 1973, October 1973, February 1974, June 1974, February 1975, June 1975, October 1977)

Trump, D. H., *Malta: an Archaeological Guide* (London 1972)

Underwood, Guy, *The Pattern of the Past* (London 1969)

Varagnac, A. and others, *L'Homme avant l'Ecriture* (Paris 1968)

Vatcher, Faith and Lance, *The Avebury Monuments* (London 1976)

Wainwright, Geoffrey, *see* Fowler, P. J. (ed.)

Watkins, Alfred, *The Ley's Hunter's Manual – a guide to early tracks sites and mark stones* (London 1925)

Watkins, Alfred, *The Ley Hunters's Manual – a guide to early tracks* (Hereford and London 1927)

Wegewitz, Willi, *Gräber der Stein – und Bronzezeit im Gebiet der Niederelbe* (Hildesheim 1949)

Wood, John Edwin, *Sun, Moon and Standing Stones* (Oxford 1978)

Wosien, Maria-Gabriele, *Sacred Dance – Encounter with the Gods* (London 1974)

Maps for finding megaliths

Balearic Islands

Sheet T26 of the 1:200 000 Mapas Turisticos, published by Firestone Hispania, covers the Balearics. An excellent Mapa Arqueologico de Menorca by J. Mascaro Pasarius is published by Miquel Cardona Florit in Ciudadela, and is widely available in Menorca.

Belgium

The Carte Belgique 1:25 000 is published by l'Institut Géographique Militaire, Brussels, and is hard to obtain except from the Institut at 3, Abbaye de la Cambre, Bruxelles. Sheet 55/1–2 (Durbuy–Mormont) covers the Wéris area in detail, though it omits one of the dolmens.

Corsica

Sheet 74, Corse Sud, of the Carte Touristique 1:100 000 series published by the Institut Geographique National of France, covers and marks Filitosa and the megaliths around Sartène.

Denmark

The Vore Fortidsminder Arkaeologisk Kort series with a scale of 1 cm to 1 km, published by the Geodaetisk Institut og Nationalmuseet, Copenhagen, are excellent large scale maps of small areas. General maps of local areas with scales of 1:100 000 and 1:50 000 are also published by the Geodaetisk Institut.

France

The 1:50 000 series published by the Institut Geographique National marks many of the important megaliths (the sheet called Auray covers the Carnac district of Brittany, but more of the monuments are marked on the sketch map in le Rouzic's guide listed in the Bibliography). The 1 : 100 000 series of the IGN and the Michelin regional maps mark some megaliths (1 : 200 000).

Germany

The Deutsche Generalkarte 1 : 200 000 series, published by Mairs Geographischer Verlag, Stuttgart, marks some major megaliths – sheet 3/4 covers the area around Bremen, including Visbek. For more detail, the incomparable 3-volume *Atlas der Megalithgräber Deutschlands* by Sprockhoff (see Bibliography) gives it all.

Great Britain

The Ordnance Survey 1 : 25 000 series marks most megaliths, though each sheet covers only a small area. The Ordnance Survey 1 : 50000 series marks the major megaliths and the sheets cover wider areas. Both series mark contours. *Stone Circles of the British Isles* by Burl (see Bibliography) has distribution maps which can be used together with the Ordnance Survey sheets. The Ordnance Survey also publishes a map of Ancient Britain in two sheets, North and South, which marks many major monuments of all Pre-Historic, Roman and Dark Age periods.

Ireland

The maps at the back of the *Guide to the National Monuments of Ireland* by Harbison (see Bibliography) mark a fair number of the important megaliths. *Stone Circles of the British Isles* by Burl (see Bibliography) has valuable distribution maps. The Ordnance Survey of Ireland 1 : 127 720 maps show many megaliths; published by the Ordnance Survey Office, Phoenix Park, Dublin.

Italy

The 1 : 200 000 series published by the Touring Club Italiano covers the Bari and Brindisi areas on sheets 20 and 21 – only a few of the dolmens are marked on these, but the maps are good and can be used with the directions found in this book. Sheets 25, 26 and 27 of the same series cover Sicily, and the rock–cut cemeteries are marked. Detailed local maps (1 : 100 000) are published by the Istituto Geografico Militare, Rome.

Malta

The Ordnance Survey series M 898 scale 1 : 25 000 covers the Maltese islands with excellent detailed contour maps, marking the temples and other megaliths clearly.

Netherlands

The Michelin 1/200 000 series covers the Low Countries, and No. 5 of that series covers the north of Holland, including the province of Drenthe where the Hunebedden are found. Many of the Hunebedden are marked on that sheet as Dolmens. Larger scale maps marking the Hunebedden are available in the 1 : 50 000 series published by the Departemente van Defensie Topografische Dienst, Delft – No. 17 (Oost) in that series covers the area from Emmen to Borger.

Portugal

The Mapas de Carreteras 1 : 500 000 series, listed under Spain, covers Portugal too, with the same reservations. The Instituto Geografico e Cadastral, Lisbon, publishes detailed area maps of 1 : 200 000, 1 : 100 000 and 1 : 50 000.

Sardinia

The 1 : 200 000 series on Italy, published by the Touring Club Italiano, covers Sardinia on sheets 28, 29 and 30. The major nuraghi and some other megaliths are marked.

Spain

The Mapas de Carreteras 1 : 500 000 series published by Firestone Hispania are decent maps which mark a few megaliths, though sometimes misleadingly. They can be used together with the distribution maps in Savory's book *Spain and Portugal* (see Bibliography). The same publisher's Mapas Turisticos series covers some coastal areas on a larger scale. The Mapa Militar de España provides sheets of local areas on scales of 1 : 50 000 and 1 : 200 000, published by the Instituto Geografico y Catastral, Madrid.

Index